The Rich Man and Lazarus

Honestly, which would you rather be, a Christian beggar or a non-Christian billionaire? How you answer shows a lot about what you really believe. Jeff Smith opens up one of Christ's most revealing teachings about life after death, and not only shows us the right answer, but gives us reasons to embrace it (and Christ) with all our hearts.

Dr. Joel R. Beeke, President, Puritan Reformed Theological Seminary, Grand Rapids, Michigan

We are told that Jonathan Edwards prayed, "Lord, stamp eternity on my eyeballs!" He wanted a pressing sense of heaven and hell—an 'eschatological edge' to his thinking, feeling, willing, preaching, and living. Jeff Smith's excellent little book will bring heaven and hell before your soul and stamp eternity on your eyeballs. With profound compassion, scriptural insight, and unflinching honesty, the author speaks directly to the reader through these pages to convince, rebuke, and exhort. In an age that too often assumes heaven and denies hell, this book provides a powerful and heartfelt corrective.

Jeremy Walker, pastor of Maidenbower Baptist Church, preacher and author

We should avail ourselves of any book, sermon, or conversation that sets the realities of eternity before us and pleads with us to respond. This brief work does just that. The book is not only doctrinal, but also pastoral and evangelistic. Although the author writes much of hell, it is clearly a means to an end—he longs for his hearers to flee from the wrath to come and embrace Christ by faith. Although this book sets forth the doctrine of hell clearly and emphatically, it is primarily a book about the gospel and the sufficiency of the Scriptures! It will convict and motivate pastors to think and preach on eternity. It will encourage believers to live their lives in the light of Christ's work and the world's need. It will warn the unconverted about the dangers of hell and instruct them in the free offer of grace. Finally, this book will be a most beneficial read for those brought up in a Christian home who demonstrate little reality of Christ.

Paul David Washer, Heartcry

Jeffery Smith is a gifted preacher and writer. In his new work, The Rich Man and Lazarus, he faithfully opens up a well-known text of Scripture and makes us to feel the realities of it in a practical and pastoral way. Here is a book to give to your unsaved friends. It is also one to read yourself. For in it, you will be edified and motivated to reach out to the lost around you. This compact volume will sit next to my all-time favorite book, An Alarm to the Unconverted, and will continually remind me to "do the work of an evangelist." I highly recommend it.

Pastor Rob Ventura, Grace Community Baptist Church, North Providence, RI, co-author of *A Portrait of Paul and Spiritual Warfare*

The Rich Man and Lazarus

The plain truth about life after death

Jeffery Smith

EP BOOKS (Evangelical Press) Registered Office: 140 Coniscliffe Road, Darlington, Co Durham DL3 7RT

www.epbooks.org
admin@epbooks.org

EP Books are distributed in the USA by:
JPL Books, 3883 Linden Ave. S.E.,
Wyoming, MI 49548

www.jplbooks.com
orders@jplbooks.com

First edition published 2019

Print ISBN 978-1-78397-245-6

British Library Cataloguing in Publication Data available

Contents

The Parable of the Rich Man and Lazarus

19 There was a certain rich man who was clothed in purple and fine linen and fared sumptuously every day.

20 But there was a certain beggar named Lazarus, full of sores, who was laid at his gate,

21 desiring to be fed with the crumbs which fell from the rich man's table. Moreover the dogs came and licked his sores.

22 So it was that the beggar died, and was carried by the angels to Abraham's bosom. The rich man also died and was buried.

23 And being in torments in Hades, he lifted up his eyes and saw Abraham afar off, and Lazarus in his bosom.

24 Then he cried and said, 'Father Abraham, have mercy on me, and send Lazarus that he may dip the tip of his finger in water and cool my tongue; for I am tormented in this flame.'

²⁵ But Abraham said, 'Son, remember that in your lifetime you received your good things, and likewise Lazarus evil things; but now he is comforted and you are tormented.

²⁶ And besides all this, between us and you there is a great gulf fixed, so that those who want to pass from here to you cannot, nor can those from there pass to us.'

²⁷ "Then he said, 'I beg you therefore, father, that you would send him to my father's house,

²⁸ for I have five brothers, that he may testify to them, lest they also come to this place of torment.'

²⁹ Abraham said to him, 'They have Moses and the prophets; let them hear them.'

³⁰ And he said, 'No, father Abraham; but if one goes to them from the dead, they will repent.'

³¹ But he said to him, 'If they do not hear Moses and the prophets, neither will they be persuaded though one rise from the dead.'

Luke 16:19–31 NKJV

Introduction

The story of the Rich Man and Lazarus contains some of the most searching and sobering words ever spoken by the Lord Jesus. The truths highlighted here, in a very vivid manner, are especially suited to awaken, sober and impress upon our minds the surpassing importance of the things of eternity and of the spiritual state of our souls before God. Jesus, the master teacher, the one who claimed to be sent to us by the Father from the world beyond, and who is embraced by Christians as the eternal Son of God, actually describes here the experience and feelings of the lost after death. He also brings before our minds several very basic and fundamental issues we can easily forget, try to avoid or not think about as often as we should. The story speaks about hell, that awful terrible place. It speaks about a division among men between those who go there and those who go to heaven. And it also has some very important things to say to us about the importance of the Bible as the means God has appointed to reveal to men the way of salvation. These are all vital issues in our day and really in every time in history.

One question often raised is whether this story is an actual history or strictly a parable. Is this a description of actual events that occurred or simply a story used to illustrate spiritual realities? Commentators have debated this, but I believe there are good reasons to understand it as both.

First, Luke never refers to the story as a parable. Usually, if not always, when Jesus tells a parable Luke specifically refers to it as a parable. In addition, Jesus introduces this story with the words, 'There was ...': *There was a certain rich man ...* and ... *there was a certain beggar.* Unlike any other parable, the Lord actually gives us the name of one of the main characters. The rich man's name is not given, perhaps out of deference to any who might have known him at the time or, perhaps, to heighten the contrast Jesus is making; the rich man's name may have been well known in the society of his day, but the story doesn't mention it. The poor man was probably unknown even to people who passed by him almost daily, but God knew him: *and there was a certain beggar named Lazarus.* All of this seems to indicate that this story is more than a parable.

On the other hand, when we come to the part of the story in which we are given a glimpse of the unseen mysteries of the spiritual world, there are certainly elements that should be understood as figurative. For example, I do not believe we are intended to understand

Jesus as teaching that the lost in hell will carry on conversations with people in heaven, such as Abraham.

Parable or a history? I believe it is both. You may come to a different conclusion, but it is important to note that this doesn't affect the lessons Jesus is teaching, as I trust we will see. Are the rich man and Lazarus actual people or are they symbolic characters who represent many multitudes like them? Either way, the message is the same.

These chapters are derived and edited from sermons first delivered by me to the congregation I serve as a pastor and not with the original purpose of written publication. Therefore, though in the context of their oral delivery, various acknowledgements were made, this material was not carefully footnoted. It is only right to acknowledge the work of others from whom I benefitted in the preparation of these messages, and to whom I am greatly indebted for some aspects of my approach to this passage, and for many of the insights opened up and developed in these pages. In addition to standard commentaries on the book of Luke, particularly helpful were *Whatever Happened to Hell?*[1] by John Blanchard; *Hell on Trial: The Case for Eternal Punishment*[2] by Robert A. Peterson; *Expository Thoughts on Luke*[3] by J.C. Ryle and especially the searching sermons of the nineteenth-century evangelist Brownlow North published as *The Rich Man and Lazarus: An Exposition of Luke 16:19–31.*[4]

Chapter One

The Contrast: Differing Conditions in This Life

First, we are introduced to the rich man. Jesus says, *There was a certain rich man who was clothed in purple and fine linen, and fared sumptuously every day.* In other words, this is the habit of his life. He is a very wealthy man who is in the habit of wearing purple and fine linen. Purple dye was extracted from a type of shellfish and it was a very expensive process in those days, so a purple outer garment, such as this rich man wore, was something mostly reserved for royalty or for the extremely rich. It was considered the royal color, the color of kings. Fine linen was also very costly. This appears to be a reference to a kind of linen produced from flax that grew on the banks of the Nile. It was a very expensive luxury item—here is a man who dressed in the finest, most extravagant and luxurious fashions of the day. He is clothed in purple and fine linen, and Jesus says, *he fared sumptuously.* The word could be translated 'splendidly, magnificently.' He lived splendidly. William Hendricksen translates it, 'living in dazzling splendor every day.' The Greek word translated 'fared' is from a verb that actually means to rejoice, or to be glad, to be merry. Literally, he is enjoying himself in splendor every day. Jesus is describing for us a man who is living the good life.

Then he contrasts the condition of this rich man with that of a poor man by the name of Lazarus. *But there was a certain beggar named Lazarus, full of sores, who was laid at his gate, desiring to be fed with the crumbs which fell from the rich man's table. Moreover, the dogs came and licked his sores.* What a contrast! Here is a man whose condition in this life is one of extreme misery. He is poor, and not only is he poor, he is afflicted. We're told he *was laid* at the rich man's gate, which suggests he suffered from some kind of disability forcing him to beg. Perhaps he is crippled, but he is also afflicted with some kind of painful disease. He is full of sores; his whole body is covered with ulcers. No doubt, he is a hard person to even look at; poor, helpless, covered with these nasty running abscesses, the filthy dogs of the street gathered around him and licking his sores. He is so helpless he could do nothing for himself. He has to be laid by others at the gate of the rich man.

Why did they lay him at the rich man's gate? Just for the very reason, the rich man is rich. He is a wealthy man and those who laid Lazarus there knew this wealthy man has the means to help Lazarus; their hope is he will have compassion if he sees this suffering, helpless, destitute man lying at his gate and will try to help him in some way.

As for Lazarus himself, he isn't looking for anything great. He is so destitute he would be content if he could just be kept from starving by the crumbs from the rich man's table. The mere scraps from the rich man's leftovers would be a great blessing to him—the stuff that's thrown out to the dogs. We aren't told if he ever received those scraps, so we can't be dogmatic, but the omission certainly gives the impression he never did. This impression is increased in the first part of this same chapter. The context is one in which Jesus has been rebuking the sin of covetousness and the neglect to make proper use of the material blessings God gives us, and I think this helps to create the impression or assumption that the rich man never really helped Lazarus, at least not in any kind of truly compassionate or substantial way. Here is the perfect opportunity for this wealthy man to show kindness and to make good use of the abundance God has provided him. Here is a man in *genuine* need, not a lazy man but one who is truly suffering and helpless. But this rich man is so caught up in living for himself he takes little notice of this poor, miserable, suffering fellow human lying at his very gate.

The conditions of these two men in this life are dramatically contrasted: the rich man living in luxury and pleasure, Lazarus in poverty and suffering. Jesus describes, secondly ...

Contrasting Deaths and Burials

So it was that the beggar died and was carried by the angels to Abraham's bosom. The rich man also died and was buried (v.22). Several facts warrant notice here.

First, they both died. With all the differences between these two men, this is one thing they both had in common and all people have in common. Unless Christ returns first, every one of us must face the grim reality of death.

But there were some striking differences concerning their deaths. We are told the rich man died and was buried, but nothing is said about Lazarus being buried. They probably just dug a hole somewhere in some forgotten place and dumped his body. By contrast, the rich man would have had a magnificent funeral. It would have been very ostentatious and expensive with the finest casket money could buy, hundreds of people there to pay their respects; a beautiful funeral oration and eulogy and a massive monument for his grave site. This leads to the third contrast.

Different Conditions Immediately After Death

Where did the two men go? Jesus tells us that Lazarus was carried by angels to Abraham's bosom. We need to understand that Jesus is describing for us the disembodied state—the state of the souls or the spirits of those who die until Christ returns and the resurrection of the body on the last day. So, of necessity, when speaking about spiritual realties, there are certain aspects of Jesus' description that are figurative. Lazarus was not physically carried in his physical body by angels. The idea is that his soul, his spirit, was escorted by angels. He was attended by angels at his death. Indeed, Hebrews 1:14 says that angels are *ministering spirits, sent forth to minister for those who will inherit salvation*. At death Lazarus was carried in spirit by the angels to Abraham's bosom, a figurative Jewish expression for heaven or paradise. The idea is that Lazarus is acknowledged as a true child of God and at his death his soul is escorted by angels into a place of conscious happiness.

Where then did the rich man go? Jesus says, *The rich man also died and was buried. And being in torments in Hades he lifted up his eyes*. The actual Greek word here is "hades." This term may sometimes be used in a general way to refer to the grave or to the abode of the dead. Also the Old Testament counterpart "sheol" may sometimes be used in this more general way. However, in both the Old and New Testaments these words are sometimes used to refer specifically to the abode of the wicked dead as a place of punishment (see for example: Psalm 9:17; Proverbs 15:24; Matthew 11:23–24). What follows makes it clear that this is how Jesus is using it here. "And *being in torments* in Hades he lifted up his eyes." The soul of the rich man went to a place of conscious torment.

To reiterate, the soul of Lazarus went to paradise, a conscious place of comfort and joy. There, the Bible teaches, the souls of the redeemed await the reuniting of the soul with a new and glorious resurrection body on the last day when Christ returns. Then begins the eternity of heaven in which our eyes will see the Lord. The soul of the rich man went to Hades, the place of torment. The Bible teaches that there the souls of the damned suffer, awaiting the final judgment when soul and body will also be reunited, both to be cast into the lake of fire to suffer God's wrath for all eternity, the state properly designated as hell.

The Lord Jesus indicates the changes Lazarus and the rich man experienced happened immediately at death. There is no time gap, no soul sleep. Lazarus died and immediately his soul went to paradise; *The rich man also died and was buried. And being in torments in Hades, he lifted up his eyes.* As soon as his eyes closed in death, he lifted up his eyes in hell. One moment he was here on earth. The next moment his soul was in a place of conscious pain and agony. The vital question is, why did they go to the places they did?

This question is very important because if we miss this we will misinterpret the meaning of this entire parable. Let me point out what was *not* the reason Lazarus went to Abraham's bosom and the rich man went to Hades. It was not because one was poor and the other was rich. Lazarus did not go to heaven because his life in this world was marked by so much suffering God thought it only fair for him to go to heaven. Nor is there something holy about being poor, in and of itself, so that men will be saved and go to heaven simply because in this life they were destitute and miserable.

Nowhere does the Bible teach this. Some poor people will go to hell. Some poor people are just as unbelieving and ungodly, and some are just as greedy and covetous, as some rich people are. It is tremendously sad to think of it, but some people live a life of misery and suffering in this world and then immediately pass from this life into torments when they die. The Bible nowhere teaches that poor people automatically go to heaven, simply because they're poor.

Furthermore, the rich man did not go into torments because he was rich. Jesus is not teaching that being rich, in and of itself, is evil and that all rich men will go to hell. If that were true, then Abraham, instead of being in heaven with Lazarus, would be in torments with the rich man because Abraham was a very rich man. If it were true that men go to hell for being rich, then David must go to hell and Joseph must also go to hell. These were men who were clothed in purple and fine linen but they were also godly men, saved men, who knew, loved and served God.

Just as being poor is not necessarily a virtue, being rich, in and of itself, is not a sin. In fact, the Scriptures teach that sometimes it's the godly man who becomes rich because of his diligence and his work ethic; because he's a good steward of his God given talents and opportunities. Indeed, the Bible assumes that *some* of God's people will be rich. Not many (1 Corinthians 1:26–29; James 2:5), but some. Paul writing to Timothy in 1 Timothy 6:17ff says, *Command those who are rich in this present age,* to give away all their possessions and repent of being rich and take a vow of poverty. Is that what he says? No, he says, *Command those who are rich in this present age, not to be haughty, nor to trust in uncertain riches.* He doesn't suggest they're sinning by being rich, he simply warns them of those sins to which the rich are especially prone. He warns them not to be conceited about it and not to trust in their riches for true happiness, security and wellbeing. *But,* he says, instead, *trust in the living God, who gives us richly all things to ...* What? *... to enjoy!* He also tells them to be generous with what God has given them, to do good with it, to have an eternal perspective in their use of it and to be ready to give and willing to share. So, there is nothing wrong, in and of itself, with being rich and enjoying the blessings God gives us when rightly gained and rightly used, though it has its peculiar temptations.

If the rich man did not go and suffer torments because he was rich, and Lazarus did not go to Abraham's bosom because he was poor, what is Jesus' point here? He makes this contrast to illustrate that our earthly temporal condition is not what really matters. It is not the outward appearance, it is our relationship to God that matters. You may be poor and afflicted in this life but if you're right with God you'll have an eternity in heaven. You may be rich in this life and enjoy all the material pleasures this world has to offer, but if you're not right with God it's all vanity, because you will spend eternity in the torments of hell. We must not interpret this parable in a way that contradicts the rest of the Bible and Jesus' teaching elsewhere.

Let's start with Lazarus. Why did Lazarus go to heaven when he died? It is true we don't merit heaven by affliction but it is also true affliction can be used of God in someone's life to have a positive effect. The psalmist could write, *Before I was afflicted I went astray, but now I have kept your word* (Psalm 119:67). Psalm 119:71 says, *It is good for me that I have been afflicted; that I might learn your statues.* Affliction doesn't save and affliction, in and of itself, is not good; it is painful and hard. But often God uses affliction to humble men and to draw them to himself. Apparently, Lazarus had learned from his affliction. He had learned that it is vain and useless for a man to seek his happiness and security in the fleeting pleasures of this life and if our hope is in this life only we are of all men most miserable. He had apparently learned that a man needs something more substantial, lasting and truly satisfying to build his hopes on; a source of peace, joy and security that can never be taken away. It was the Lord by his Spirit who taught him that and, no doubt, one of the ways he was taught it was in the school of affliction.

He was also taught to see his own sinfulness—to see his need of mercy and forgiveness, his need of a Savior. Having his eyes opened to these realities he turned to

God to put his hope in those things that are unseen and eternal. He put his trust in the Christ to come, as revealed in the Old Testament Scriptures. He fled in faith to the promised Messiah for refuge to lay hold upon the hope that is set before us in the gospel. Lazarus was a repentant, believing man. He was a man born of the Spirit and joined to Christ by faith and that is why he was in a place of happiness after death.

You might ask where that is in the text, and you could ask by what authority I say Lazarus went to a place of happiness? My answer is on the basis of the highest authority of all: the infallible, inerrant and absolute authority of God's Holy Word. He went to Abraham's bosom, a place that would be a heaven to him while he awaited the resurrection of the body. The Bible tells us very plainly that no man goes to heaven but through Christ. Jesus said, *No one comes to the Father except through Me* (John 14:6). *Nor is there salvation in any other, for there is no other name under heaven given among men by which we must be saved* (Acts 4:12): the Lord Jesus Christ only is the way. Lazarus was saved. Therefore, we can know that he came to God through Christ. Brownlow North puts it so well:

> Anything may take a man to Christ. A rich man may feel as Solomon felt: that this world can be no satisfying portion, and the thought may take him to Christ. A poor man may feel as Lazarus felt: that this world can be no satisfying portion, and the thought may take him to Christ. Prosperity, adversity, health, sickness, joy,

THE CONTRAST: DIFFERING CONDITIONS IN THIS LIFE

sorrow, the fall of a leaf, or the flight of a bird, anything, everything, no matter what, may be made effectual to this end, in the hands of God the Spirit. There is nothing that may not take a man to Christ, but there is nothing but Christ can take a man to heaven.[5]

If Lazarus went to eternal happiness it must be because he was led by God's Spirit to repent of sin and to put his faith in Christ.

If this is so, then why did the rich man go to hell? The rich man went to hell because of his sin and unbelief. We don't even have to deduce this, the passage tells us. Jesus gives us a picture of the rich man in torments in which we have a conversation between him and Abraham. Here the root of his problem is revealed. He would not be persuaded of the truth.

> Then he said, 'I beg you therefore, father, that you would send him to my father's house, for I have five brothers that he may testify to them, lest they also come to this place of torment.' Abraham said to him, 'They have Moses and the prophets; let them hear them.' And he said, 'No, father Abraham; but if one goes to them from the dead, they will repent.' But he said to him, 'If they do not hear Moses and the prophets, neither will they be persuaded though one rise from the dead.' (Luke 16:27ff)

You see, this was the root of the rich man's problem and why he was lost. While he was still in this world, while he still had time to be converted, he would not be persuaded. He had the Scriptures, he had Moses and the prophets, but he refused to believe them. He would not repent. He was content to live without God, to live a life in which he lived for this world alone. He lived for the fleeting pleasures of the moment and in this way of life he had become so selfish and self-preoccupied he had little or no concern for the sufferings of his fellow man. Instead of using the wealth God had so blessed him with to serve God and to minister to others, he kept it all to himself. He had everything a man could want in this world and, though being rich, in and of itself, is not sinful, his prosperity kept him blinded to his spiritual need. He felt secure and self-satisfied. Like the rich man in another of our Lord's parables, *he said to himself 'Soul, you have many goods laid up for many years; take your ease; eat, drink, and be merry.' But God said to him, 'Fool! This night your soul will be required of you; then whose will those things be which you have provided?'* (Luke 12:19–20). That was the end of his foolish charade of self deception. He died and went to torment and he is still there today and he will be lost for all eternity. Oh, what a sad, awful, heart-breaking consideration!

Lesson 1: A Man's Condition in This Life is No Certain Sign of Where He Stands Before God.

Jesus' teaching tells us that a man or woman may be very rich and prosperous in this life only to go to torment when he or she dies. A person may be very poor or very afflicted with suffering in this life, only to go to eternal happiness when he or she dies. A vital lesson from this is that we must not judge by outward appearance. There is an attitude that says, 'Well, if you really want to have a growing, prosperous, influential church, you need to put your building in an upper middle class neighborhood or a high class neighborhood. You need to focus all your outreach and your church programs on reaching white collar people and those who are well off.' It seems few think about planting a church in a poor neighborhood. 'There's no use trying to reach out in a place like that. The stable, respectable, intelligent people who have money live out in the new housing developments.' As a result, perhaps we get excited when 'the right kind of person' starts coming to our church but not so much when a poor person comes. We should remember the words in James 2:1ff:

> My brethren, do not hold the faith of our Lord Jesus Christ, the Lord of glory, with partiality. For if there should come into your assembly a man with gold rings, in fine apparel, and there should also come in a poor man in filthy clothes, and you pay attention to the one wearing the fine clothes and say to him, 'You sit here in a good place,' and say to the poor man, 'You stand there' ... have you not shown partiality ... Listen, my beloved brethren; Has not God chosen the poor of this world to be rich in faith, and heirs of the kingdom which He has promised to them that love Him.

We must remember what our Lord teaches us in this parable. A man's outward condition in this life is no certain sign of where he stands in his relationship to God. Many of those God has purposed in eternity to save come from among the poor. Let us not despise them.

Lesson 2: When Men Die They Do Not Cease to Exist or Enter into a State of Soul Sleep.

Some believe death is the end: you die and that's it. Others, who do believe in the final resurrection of *the body* at the last day, argue that until that time the souls of the dead are asleep. There is no consciousness of the soul after death. At death we enter into a state they call soul sleep, or limbo. Jesus indicates here the fallacy of both of these notions. When men die they do not cease to exist and they do not enter into a state of unconscious soul sleep either. Lazarus died and his soul was carried into Abraham's bosom. The rich man died and his soul was in a conscious state of torment.

The Scriptures teach that the soul of the believer at death immediately goes into the presence of God. Christ said to the thief on the cross who repented and believed, *Today you will be with Me in Paradise* (Luke 23:43). Paul could write in 2 Corinthians 5:8, *We are confident I say, and willing rather to be absent from the body, and to be present with the Lord* (KJV). For the Christian to be absent from the body is to be present with the Lord, a truth which should be a great source of comfort to God's people. When we think about our saved loved ones and friends who have gone before us, where are they now? Have they ceased to exist? Are they in some unconscious state of limbo? No, they are in the presence of the Lord Jesus Christ. They are with the Lord in that place the Bible calls Paradise. If you have trusted the Lord Jesus Christ to save you, when your own last hour comes and you lay down to die, you're about to breathe your last breath in this world and to step out into the unknown, this text tells you the angels will be there to transport your soul safely into that blessed place where sin and sorrow will be no more. And there you will be with Christ.

But what happens to the unconverted when they die? The Scriptures teach that the souls of the lost enter into a state of conscious torment and punishment. We're told in Acts 1:25 that Judas, the son of perdition, when he died, went to his own place. He didn't cease to exist. He went to a place that was prepared for him and for all like him. And being the son of perdition that place was perdition. His soul went into torment. 1 Peter 3:19 speaks of the spirits of unconverted men being in prison. They are in a state of imprisonment awaiting the final judgment. 2 Peter 2:9 compares the condition of all the unrighteous dead to that of the fallen angels and it tells us they are being reserved under punishment for the Day of Judgment.

Oh, how awful to think of it! How can we even mention it without tears? The intermediate state for the lost is a state of conscious existence. It is a place of imprisonment, a place of punishment, and, as Jesus tells us here, it is a place of torment. And it is a place into which they enter immediately at death. They have no hope of ever escaping. The only thing they have to look forward to is a day which they greatly dread; the last day, the resurrection of the body and the judgment to come which will only result in the intensification of their misery. For then, not only their souls will suffer in hell, but, according to Scripture both body and soul together will suffer torment throughout the ages of eternity.

This is the teaching of Scripture. This is the loving Lord Jesus Christ himself who tells us this. To anyone reading this who is not a Christian, or you have no scripturally-based assurance that through Christ you've been delivered from this awful end, my plea to you is very simple. Flee from the wrath to come before it's too late. Death is coming to all of us. It's coming to you, my friend, unless Christ returns first. You can ignore it. You can try not to think about it but it's going to happen anyway. You have no promise of tomorrow. You could die today and then it will be too late to repent, too late to pray, to believe. There will be no more opportunity, no more mercy. Will you not stop on your path to hell? Will you not turn and run to Christ?

The good news of the gospel is that you don't have to go to hell. Jesus stands ready to receive you and to save you. He has offered up himself as the atonement for sin upon the cross. God has raised him from the dead testifying to the sufficiency of that atonement. *God so loved the world that He gave His only begotten Son, that whoever believes in Him should not perish ...* (John 3:16). My friend, seek the Lord while he may be found. Turn to him in faith. Call upon him now while he is near, before it's too late. He will hear you and have mercy upon you.

Chapter Two

The Place and the Pains

We are living in a day in which the concept of hell and eternal punishment is either denied, ridiculed or ignored. Modern writer John Blanchard, commenting on this, has written, 'At some point in the nineteen-sixties hell disappeared. No one could say for certain when this happened. First it was there, then it wasn't.' In his book, *Whatever Happened to Hell?* Blanchard tells us that the American church historian Martin Marty, professor at the University of Chicago Divinity School, when preparing a Harvard lecture on the subject of hell, consulted the indexes of several scholarly journals dating back over a period of a hundred years to 1888 and failed to find a single entry about hell. His conclusion was, 'Hell disappeared and no one noticed.' Gordon Kaufman, a professor at Harvard Divinity School said that hell has been in decline for 400 years and is now so diminished that the process is irreversible: 'I don't think there can be any future for hell.'

Again, quoting from John Blanchard, he points out that, 'This retreat is reflected in theological literature. One volume of Christian doctrine, with nearly 800 pages, and edited by three highly respected Christian leaders, has only eight lines on hell.' Eight hundred pages of Christian doctrine and only eight lines of the book refer to the subject of hell. Blanchard goes on to point out that this is eight lines more about hell than is found in another major work entitled *Handbook of Contemporary Theology*. That book has not even one line given to the subject of hell.[6]

Indeed, hell is almost a forgotten subject in our day, and I am sure the devil likes it that way. Admittedly, it's not a pleasant subject. It is hard to speak about it. It opens us up to being misunderstood and to being accused of being unloving and unkind. Hell is made fun of in popular culture. This is part of the temptation to neglect it, but we must not do so. Hell is a subject Christ himself and the rest of the New Testament repeatedly puts before us. If you believe the Bible, love will prevent you from making a joke of hell or neglecting it.

In the last chapter we considered vv.19–23 of Luke chapter 16, where the different conditions of a lost rich man and a saved poor man are described and contrasted by the Lord Jesus. In the remainder of the account, vv.23–31, we listen to a conversation with a man in torment, a conversation in which his tormented pleas and arguments are rejected. There are two pleas he makes and in this chapter we will begin to consider the first one.

What was the first plea of the man in hell? He pleads for water to cool his tongue.

> And being in torments in Hades, he lifted up his eyes and saw Abraham afar off, and Lazarus in his bosom. Then he cried and said, 'Father Abraham, have mercy on me, and send Lazarus that he may dip the tip of his finger in water and cool my tongue; for I am tormented in this flame.' (vv.23–24)

Before we begin to look at this, I think it is wise to give a word of caution. We have to remember, as I said in the last chapter, Jesus is beginning to describe for us the disembodied state; the condition of the souls of men after death, prior to the reuniting of the soul and body at the resurrection on the last day. The Bible teaches that at the resurrection the spirits of both believers and unbelievers will be reunited with their bodies. Then believers will enjoy the glories of heaven and the new earth, both body and soul. Unbelievers, by contrast, will experience the pains of hell in both body and soul. But Jesus is not describing here the bodily condition of the damned after the resurrection. He is describing the condition of their souls, or spirits, after death and before the resurrection. The rich man died and was buried. His body was placed in the grave to await the resurrection of the unjust on the last day. But, though his body was placed in the grave to await that day, his soul went immediately into torment at the moment of his

death. I point this out to help us to see that, of necessity
then, there are elements of our Lord's description that
are figurative. Why? Because he's speaking about the
unseen, nonphysical, spiritual realm. For example, a
spirit or soul doesn't have a literal physical finger to dip
into water, or a literal physical tongue to be cooled by
a drop of water. The soul doesn't drink physical water.
We need to understand that Jesus is describing for us
in physical terms, the spiritual sufferings of the souls of
the damned in torment. The failure to realize this has
resulted in all kinds of strange conclusions being drawn
from this parable.

For example, I don't think we're warranted to draw the
conclusion from this that Jesus is intending to teach that
the souls in heaven and the souls in hell are in the same
general location, or that they will be able to carry on
conversations with each other. Also, as was pointed out
in the last chapter, Abraham's bosom was a figurative
Jewish expression for Paradise. Therefore, when Lazarus
is depicted as actually being in the literal physical
bosom of the Old Testament saint Abraham, who is
then depicted as carrying on a conversation with the
man in torment, we are not to conclude from this that
happiness is actually found somewhere in Abraham's
literal physical bosom.

This is not to say that what Jesus teaches in this parable
is untrue or that it is unclear to a careful and willing
reader. Nevertheless, we have to be careful to separate
the realities portrayed from the figurative aspects of

the form in which our Lord portrays them. How do we do that? We can only do that by being very careful to interpret the details of the parable in a manner consistent with the teaching of the rest of Scripture on this subject.

To be clear, we must not forget that even those aspects that are figurative are still intended to illustrate for us very real and literal truths. It's not that the reality depicted is something less than the figurative terms used to describe it, quite the opposite, the reality is something more. The reason figurative terms are sometimes used is that the reality confounds the ability of human language to describe them adequately, or the reality is beyond our present ability fully to comprehend. Jesus is now taking us into the world of spirits, the unseen realm. He's depicting for us the spiritual condition, sufferings, concerns, feelings, sensations and longings of the spirits of the damned. And he does so in terms and pictures that do, indeed, accurately present these realities but in a way we can understand. We come now to the first plea of the man in hell.

The Condition Giving Rise to His Plea

There are basically two things we're told about his condition. We have the place to which his soul was consigned and we have the pains to which his soul was subjected.

The Place to Which His Soul Was Consigned

We read that the rich man died and was buried, *And being in torments in Hades, he lifted up his eyes.* The place to which his soul was consigned at death was this place called Hades. I want to emphasize here that Hades is described as a place, not merely a state of mind. As mentioned before, Acts 1:25 says that Judas, the son of perdition as he is called elsewhere, *went to his own place.* After death, Judas did not cease to exist. His soul went to a place and, being the son of perdition, we know the place to which he went was perdition. He went to Hades. The Bible consistently refers to hell as a place. The Bible tells us nothing of its precise location, nothing of its size or its dimensions. As someone has suggested, it may very well be a place beyond our time-and-space understanding. Nevertheless, the Bible does make it clear that it is a place; not merely a state of mind or a philosophical concept. This should be obvious, for not only do *the souls* of the damned suffer, the Scriptures tell us that, after the resurrection, they will suffer hell in both body and soul. Now for both the body and soul to be punished in hell, there must be an actual place where this is done. And though we aren't given a detailed description of this place, it is pictured for us in Scripture by several different places to which it is compared.

First of all, one of the most common words used to describe this place is the Greek word *Gehenna.* Jesus uses this word no fewer than eleven times to describe the eternal destiny of the lost. Where did the word come from? It was the Greek name of a place called the valley of Hinnom. The Jewish name was *Ge Hinnom*. The valley of Hinnom was a deep, narrow ravine outside the city of Jerusalem. It was notorious in Jewish history as a place where idolatrous kings had offered human sacrifices to pagan idols, until King Josiah put an end to that during his reign. After that, according to some later sources, it may have become the sewage cesspool of the city. Later Gehenna was used to refer to the place where the damned are eternally punished, and Jesus used the word in this way.

Secondly, hell is also compared in Scripture to a prison. In the parable of the King's servant who was cast into prison for refusing to forgive his fellow servant, Jesus gave this warning in Matthew 18:35, *So My heavenly Father also will do to you, if each of you, from his heart, does not forgive his brother his trespasses.* You too, he says, will be cast into prison. If we understand him as referring to a punishment beyond the grave, he is comparing hell to a prison. Now, granted, some may interpret the reference in Matthew 18:35 to some kind of temporal punishment. There is, however, another text where hell seems to be even more clearly in view and is compared to a prison. In 1 Peter 3:19 those in hell are described as the spirits prison.

Thirdly, hell is also described in Scripture as a place of fire. We see it here in this parable. The rich man cried, *Send Lazarus that he may dip the tip of his finger in water and cool my tongue; for I am tormented in this flame.* There is this reference to fire. Psalm 11:6 says *Upon the wicked He will rain coals; Fire and brimstone and a burning wind shall be the portion of their cup.* In the last verse of Isaiah, God has a very sobering message for all those who rebel against his authority. *For their worm dies not, and their fire is not quenched. They shall be an abhorrence to all flesh* (Isaiah 66:24). The prophet Nahum uses similar language speaking of God's judgment of the wicked in Nahum 1:6, *Who can stand before His indignation and who can abide the fierceness of His anger? His fury is poured out like fire.* Jesus said, in the Sermon on the Mount, *But whoever says, 'You fool!', shall be in danger of hell fire.* Over and over he describes hell as a place of fire. He says in Matthew 18:8, *If your hand or your foot causes you to sin, cut it off and cast it from you. It is better for you to enter into life lame or maimed, rather than having two hands or two feet to be cast into the everlasting fire.* He describes hell in Matthew 25:41 as a place of eternal fire prepared for the devil and his angels. In the book of the Revelation, hell is described as a lake burning with fire and brimstone. For example, we read in Revelation 20:15, *And anyone not found written in the Book of Life was cast into the lake of fire.*

There is much we may not know about hell, but one thing the Bible is very clear about, hell is a place. It is a real place. What kind of a place is it? It is a place of eternal punishment. It's compared to a prison and to a lake that burns with fire and brimstone. So, there is this awful place to which the rich man's soul was consigned.

The Pains to Which His Soul Was Subjected

Let me preface this by expressing my own personal horror when considering how the Bible describes the pains of hell. It is not with a kind of sadistic glee that I open this up. May God help me to never speak or write about hell without a broken heart and without a deeply felt compassion for my fellow human beings who are in danger of going there. Indeed, the Bible tells us these things for our good that we might be caused to seek the way of deliverance that God himself has provided.

We are told at the beginning of v.23 that, *being in torments in hell he lifted up his eyes.* Then we have the man's own words in v.24. *Send Lazarus, that he may dip the tip of his finger in water, and cool my tongue,* Why? *for I am tormented in this flame.* We read in Revelation 14:10ff that, *he himself shall also drink of the wine of the wrath of God, which is poured out full strength into the cup of His indignation. He shall be tormented with fire and brimstone in the presence of the holy angels and in the presence of the Lamb. And the smoke of their torment ascends forever and ever; and they have no rest day or night.* This word 'torment' refers to severe and conscious suffering. Hell is a place of great pain. The Scriptures use the most graphic language possible to describe the torments of hell.

But what do the pains of hell consist of? Here we have to be very careful to stick to what the Scriptures tell us and not try to conjecture beyond that. The pains and torments of hell as God describes them in his Word certainly are so horrible we could never describe them as worse than they really are. But at the same time, we have to be content with what God has chosen to reveal. So how does the Bible describe the punishment and the pains of hell?

First of all, hell is a place of banishment and separation. Jesus tells us the lost will be cast into outer darkness. He describes hell as being cast away, being banished into what is called outer darkness. The Scripture says Jesus will say to them, *Depart from Me, you cursed* (Matthew 25:41). Again, the idea is of separation and banishment.

This aspect of hell is referred to in many other places. Matthew 8:12 speaks of the lost being *cast out* into outer darkness. Jesus speaks of them *going away* into everlasting punishment. Paul in 2 Thessalonians 1:9 says unbelievers will be punished with everlasting destruction *from the presence of the Lord* and from the glory of his power. They are shut out from the presence and the glory of the Lord. It's not that the presence of God won't be in hell, in the absolute sense. God is everywhere all the time and his presence will be in hell and his presence will be painfully felt in hell. That will be part of what makes hell, hell for the damned. God's anger and his wrath will be keenly felt in hell. But the idea is that the lost will be cut off from his gracious presence and from the glories of our Lord's heavenly kingdom. They will be banished, separated, from all the blessings of God's common grace they enjoyed in this life.

You see, whatever is truly good in this life that even lost men and women experience and enjoy is there and experienced by them because of the indulgence of God's common grace. It is because of God's longsuffering and kindness, even toward his enemies. God allows men, women, young people, boys and girls who ignore him and are opposed to him, to enjoy the good things he has created. As Jesus said, *He makes His sun to rise on the evil and on the good, and He sends His rain on the just and on the unjust* (Matthew 5:45). Such are God's dealings with the lost in this life. He is longsuffering and patient with them. They still receive a great deal of innocent enjoyment out of life. They enjoy good food, drink, sport, music, art, laughter, friendship and the blessings of family relationships. Some of them enjoy nice homes and a soft bed.

But, my dear friend, all of that will come to an end in hell. If you are not saved you'll be stripped of the good things God has allowed you to enjoy in this life. You'll be stripped of all good whatever. All manifestations of God's kindness and common grace toward you will be cut off and you'll be banished into what the Bible calls outer darkness. You'll be banished from the love of God, banished from the goodness of God, banished from the patience of God and from the mercy of God, banished from anything from God that could bring any benefit to you or even a moment's pleasure to you. There will not even be one drop of water to cool your tongue. All will be taken away. You'll also be separated from all the joys and blessings that could have been yours in heaven and in the world to come. Heaven will be forfeited forever. It will be too late to seek the Lord.

Surely this must be one of the agonies of the damned in hell. The thought of what they might have had and where they could be, if they had not been so foolish as to refuse to seek the Lord while he may be found; if they had not been so foolish as to be content to live without God; if they had sought the Lord and had given themselves no rest until they were saved by him and belonged to him as one of his children. But they squandered all of their opportunities and now they realize what might have been, if they had not been so sinfully foolish.

We see this hinted at here in Jesus' description of the rich man in hell—he is in torment but at the same time he sees Lazarus in Abraham's bosom. He is conscious of the glories and blessings that he missed. Indeed, Jesus tells us in Luke 13:28, *There will be weeping and gnashing of teeth, when you see Abraham and Isaac and Jacob and all the prophets in the kingdom of God, and yourselves thrust out.*

There may be someone reading these words and, if you continue as you are, you may feel the pain of seeing your mother received into heaven but yourself thrust out. Your dear father in heaven, your dear brother in heaven, your precious sister who was always so kind to you. In a sense you 'see' your saved loved ones in heaven but you yourself thrust out, banished and forever forgotten, cast out into God's cosmic trash dump and eternally separated from any good.

Secondly, hell is a place of terrible inward torments of the soul. Isn't this the essence of what we see here in this parable of the rich man and Lazarus? Remember here we see the intermediate state before the body is rejoined to the soul at the resurrection. The rich man died and immediately he lifted up his eyes, the eyes of his soul as we might say, and he found he was in hell. His disembodied soul was in torment. Clearly in this context the agony described is a spiritual agony—an agony of the soul.

What are some of those inward soul agonies the damned experience in hell? Well, again, we have to be cautious here. What does the Bible warrant us to say? One I've already mentioned is the agony of regret over what might have been. But there are other agonies of the soul the Scriptures imply.

First, there's the torment of a fully awakened conscience. As we'll see in the next chapter, the rich man was called to remember the way he had lived his life on earth. This implies that the souls of the damned remember. Jesus says in Mark 9:48, speaking of those in hell, *their worm dies not and the fire is not quenched.* What does he mean by that? Blanchard points out that the text does not simply say 'worm' but *their* worm. The Lord is speaking of internal suffering, their worm, a worm, as it were, within their own soul. As one of the old writers put it, 'Not only will the unbeliever be in hell, but hell will be in him too.' This suggests that the worm very likely refers to the sinner's conscience.

There are few things more painful than a fully awakened guilty conscience. In Shakespeare's *Richard*

III, the king is nearly paralyzed with guilt. He cries out, 'My conscience hath a thousand several tongues. And every tongue brings in a several tale. And every tale condemns me for a villain.' Indeed, the pangs of an awakened conscience can be almost unbearable *in this life*. But the pangs of conscience in hell will surely be much greater.

It seems this will especially be the case after the final judgment. I say that because at the judgment God will expose and convince men of their sins. We read in Jude 15 that God will, *execute judgment on all, to convict all who are ungodly among them of all their ungodly deeds which they have committed in an ungodly way, and of all the harsh things which ungodly sinners have spoken against Him.* God will vindicate himself in punishing them. The Greek word translated 'convict' in that text is a word that means to prove to be wrong. God will prove sinners to be wrong, he will convict their consciences. That's not the same as saying their hearts will be changed and they'll experience a true repentance. No, but their consciences will be convicted and God will prove them to be in the wrong. This implies that the conscience will be alive in hell. And there will be no amusements, no drugs, no alcohol, no internet, no cell phone, no TV to distract the mind in the effort to stifle conviction. In the words of John Flavel, 'Conscience which should have been the sinner's curb on earth, becomes the whip that must lash his soul in hell.'

Hell will be a place of absolute, complete hopelessness and despair; an unbearable, unending depression. As we will see later, the Scripture teaches that there is no escape and no end to the torments of hell for the damned. Therefore, there is no hope in hell. What terrible, horrible despair the damned must feel. The despair of knowing there is no hope. The suffering has no end.

I think there is also warrant to believe that there will be the agony of unfulfilled desires. The soul will still be the soul. It will still have its desires but none will be fulfilled. And the souls of the damned will still be unrenewed souls, unregenerate souls, in bondage to sin and corruption. Hell, as we will see, is not remedial, it is punitive. It doesn't change men's hearts and make them holy. They'll still be the same unrenewed souls in bondage to sin as they were. There will be the agony of sinful lusts and passions still raging in the souls of the damned.

Seven times in the New Testament Jesus describes hell as a place of weeping and gnashing of teeth. Weeping speaks of the emotion of deep sorrow. The exact word Jesus uses in those expressions literally means to wail, not merely to shed some tears, but to weep and to wail. The picture is that of someone convulsing in an uncontrollable expression of grief and anguish.

But the phrase 'gnashing of teeth' conveys another emotion. As we look at how this idea is used in Scripture, it's actually used to describe passionate anger. For example, when Stephen was stoned to death in Acts, we are told that the Jews, when they heard his sermon, were furious and gnashed their teeth at him. This is the thought conveyed when Jesus says in hell there will be gnashing of teeth.

> In hell, that anger will be more intense than any this world has ever seen. The wicked will be angry at the things which gave them pleasure on earth but now give them pain in hell; angry at the sins that wrecked their lives; angry at themselves for being who they are; angry at Satan and his helpers for producing the temptations which led them into sin; and, even while compelled to acknowledge his glory and goodness (and justness), angry at God for condemning them to this dreadful fate.[7]

Hell is a place of banishment and separation. Hell is a place of terrible inward torments of the soul.

Thirdly, hell is a place of the active inflicting of God's wrath upon the sinner. Men are separated from God in hell in the sense of being separated from his goodness and mercy and his common grace. But they are not separated from God's wrath—God will be in hell just as he is everywhere all the time. This will be the worst of the terrors of the damned. John writes in Revelation 14:10 that they will be tormented with fire and brimstone ... *in the presence of the Lamb.*

The Scriptures speak of separation in two ways. There is separation in terms of distance and separation in terms of relationship. Those in hell will be separated from God forever in terms of relationship, but in terms of distance, they will still be in God's presence. They will sense and feel and experience the wrath of God. That wrath is described in Scripture as a burning fire. *Our God is a consuming fire* (Hebrews 13:29). *His wrath is poured out like fire* (Nahum 1:6). Those in Hell are said to *drink of the wine of the wrath of God which is poured out without measure.*

I will mention one more aspect of the sufferings of the souls in hell, even though it is painful to continue this theme. To be true to Scripture, there's something else that needs to be mentioned

Fourthly, there is the torment of anticipating even worse that is yet to come. You see, all these things I have been describing are spiritual torments of the soul. But the souls of the lost in torment now also have suffering of the body to look forward to at the resurrection, when what we may call the full reality of hell begins. Things don't get better there, they only get worse. The Scripture says on that day the body and soul will be reunited to stand before Christ in the final judgment, and then the body and soul together will be cast into the lake of fire.

Men sin against God in their bodies, as well as within their souls. Man, as a being, is a body-soul entity. Therefore, it is the whole man who will be punished, body as well as soul, in the final state. Jesus says in John 5:29 that the resurrection will be a resurrection of the bodies of both the just and the unjust. According to Daniel 12:2, at the resurrection the bodies of some will be raised to everlasting life, while those of others will be raised to shame and everlasting contempt. So, just as believers will be glorified body and soul, the lost, even in their bodies, will bear the hideous marks of their moral and spiritual deformity. And they will be damned and tormented forever both body and soul.

This is not a very pleasant subject, but it is in the Bible and we cannot ignore it if we love the Word of God. We have to reckon with it. Christ warns us about this place called hell for our good. He warns sinners about this place because he loves us and he came to save us.

Lessons

Let me speak frankly to anyone reading this book who is outside of Christ or who has no scriptural assurance that through Christ you have been delivered from this awful fate. Your heart has never been changed from the heart you were born with and received from your father Adam. You have never been awakened to see yourself as a lost sinner headed for judgment. You have never sought the Lord for mercy and found that mercy in Jesus Christ. My friend, you're in danger of this hell the Bible describes. The Scriptures tell us that the only way you can escape this awful damnation of eternal torment is through personal faith in Jesus Christ as your Lord and Savior. You must enter in through the narrow gate that leads to life; the narrow gate of conversion to Christ. This gate is only entered by repentance from sin, and by faith in the Lord Jesus. It is a gate that cannot be entered by twos or by threes. You must enter it alone for yourself.

This gate is still open, dear friend. It's not too late yet. Christ is warning you as you read these pages and he is also telling you that he stands ready to receive you and to save you. God sent his Son to die on the cross for sinners. He took the wrath sinners deserve and was punished in their place so that all who repent from going their own way, and from being their own lord, and look to him for mercy shall be saved. Oh, that you would run to Christ this day to lay hold of the hope of the gospel.

But now I would address myself to any of God's people who may be reading these pages. Let us be moved by these things to have a greater burden for the lost. We say that we believe the Bible. How can we believe it and see so many souls around us—men, women and children in our communities and throughout the world, and even in our own families sitting at our own tables ... How can we see them tottering on the brink of this awful doom, and not be moved with compassion, and have tears fill our eyes at times? What are you doing, what am I doing, to rescue the souls of the perishing? Where are our prayers and our fastings? Where are our agonizing intercessions? Where is our compassion? Where are our tears? Where are our words of gospel witness? Where is your sacrificial giving of your money, your time? Where are you contributing your efforts, in accordance with your particular talents, opportunities, station and calling in life, to the great work of taking the gospel to every person? Surely, in light of these things, we are all at best half awake, or half asleep. I feel sometimes that I do not feel; that my heart is so hard and cold. May God help us, may God help me, and fill me with greater love and compassion for my fellow man.

Chapter Three

Prayer Too Late

I remind you of the emphasis in the last chapter: Jesus is describing for us the disembodied state; the condition of the souls of men after death prior to the reuniting of the soul and body at the resurrection on the last day. The rich man died and was buried. His body was placed in the grave to await the resurrection of the unjust on the last day, when both body and soul reunited will be cast into hell. But, though his body was placed in the grave, his soul went immediately into torment at the moment of his death. Obviously, as was noted earlier, there are elements of our Lord's description that are figurative since he is speaking about the unseen, nonphysical, spiritual realm. Jesus is describing for us in physical terms, and in very vivid earthly terms, the spiritual sufferings of the souls of the damned in hell. The details must be interpreted in a manner consistent with the rest of Scripture on this subject. But we must also remember that even those parts that are figurative are intended to communicate certain realities.

We are now ready to continue our consideration of the first plea of the man in hell. In the last chapter we considered the condition giving rise to the man's plea. Now I want us to consider the content of his plea in terms of its manner, its irony, its description and its problem.

The Manner of His Address

The rich man addresses Abraham in this way: *Father Abraham, have mercy on me* (v.24). The Jews considered it the greatest of honors to have Abraham as their father. To have Abraham as your father was to be a child of the covenant, a member of the old covenant people of God. And, indeed, this man was a physical descendant of Abraham. He was born an Israelite. Perhaps, as typical of the Jews in our Lord's day, he had drawn great comfort from this. He was not as other men are in the world, certainly not a Gentile pagan. Like every good Jewish boy, he had been circumcised on the eighth day. He was a son of the old covenant church. But though he was a son of the church, he was not a son of God. Yes, he was of the seed of Abraham according to the flesh, but not according to the Spirit. As we read in Romans 9:6, *They are not all Israel, who are of Israel* or in Galatians 3:26 and 29, *For you are all sons of God through faith in Christ Jesus; And if you are Christ's, then you are Abraham's seed, and heirs according to the promise.* This man was a physical descendant of Abraham and, therefore, a beneficiary of all the outward religious privileges of that relationship, but he was not a spiritual descendant of Abraham by faith in the salvation of God, promised through the Christ to come. Nevertheless, here he appeals to his external relationship with Abraham.

This was typical of the Jews of that day. There was a tendency to think that the mere possession of outward covenant privilege, and being a physical descendant of Abraham, somehow placed them in good stead in their relationship to God. Jesus was fond of blowing that deception out of the water, and he does so here. Here we see a child of Abraham in hell.

We sometimes see this same kind of attitude today. There are people who think that because their parents are Christians, or because they live in a so-called Christian nation, or because they attend church and have been baptized, this means that all is well with their souls. They put their hope in outward religious privileges. But here we're reminded there will be sons of the church in hell.

The Irony of His Plea

What does the word irony mean? One definition is this: it's a combination of circumstances, or a result, the exact opposite of what might be expected. Now that death has come for both Lazarus and the rich man, the tables have completely turned. This rich man, who apparently never showed any mercy toward Lazarus when the poor fellow was lying at his gate covered in sores, is now in the position of begging mercy from him. We also see how low the rich man has been brought and just how awful his misery in hell is. He doesn't ask for anything great, just a little drop of water; one little drop of water from the finger of that old dirty beggar covered with sores who used to lie at his gate. In his earthly life the rich man had all the comforts money could afford; he lived in splendor every day, eating the best foods, drinking the best wines. Now he is so miserable he would gladly give all his wealth, if he could, just to have one little drop of water from the finger of that old dirty beggar he so often ignored. But in hell all mercy is ended and there is not even the smallest little drop. There is no relief, not a drop of pity from God for those in hell. In this life, God grants to us his common grace, giving us good things to enjoy and sparing us what our sins deserve. He also graciously and freely offers saving mercy to sinners in Christ. But in hell it will be too late.

The Description of His Plea

Brownlow North very searchingly draws attention to three things in the description of his plea.

First, we are told the man in torment saw something he had never seen in this life. Luke 16:23 says *And being in torments in Hades he lifted up his eyes, and saw Abraham afar off, and Lazarus in his bosom.* He saw Lazarus in the kingdom of heaven. He not only saw and felt the torments of hell to which he was now subjected, he also saw something of the heaven from which he was now excluded. Again, a soul doesn't have literal physical eyes and exactly how a soul can see may be something of a mystery to us. But not entirely: Jesus may be illustrating a spiritual sight of some kind, a spiritual perception. This man in hell could see, that is, he could perceive and understand something of what he had missed.

The Bible says *Eye has not seen, nor ear heard, nor have entered into the heart of man, the things which God has prepared for those who love Him. But God has revealed them to us* (that is to us who have been born again, who are Christians) *through His Spirit* (1 Corinthians 2:9–10). Believers have tasted of the glories of the world to come in this life. Our spiritual eyes, once blinded by sin, have been opened and granted a spiritual perception to see our desperate need and our lost condition and to behold the glory of God in the face of Jesus Christ. We have been enabled by the Holy Spirit to recognize something of the surpassing value of those things which are eternal. We have been caused to see in Christ, and in the salvation in him, the pearl of great price, as Jesus describes it in one of his parables. The pearl of all-surpassing value that, when once a man sees it, he is willing to sell all that he has, if need be, to possess it. The Christian is one who has caught a glimpse of that now and his heart and his life have been changed by it. He now counts all things but loss, but dung, in comparison to the excellence of the knowledge of Christ Jesus his Lord (Philippians 3:8ff).

But no man ever sees this unless he is born of the

Spirit. As Jesus said, *Except a man be born again, he cannot see the kingdom of God* (John 3:3, KJV). The word 'see' doesn't speak merely of being a visual spectator of something. It speaks of intelligent understanding and perception and appreciation. We often use the word 'see' in this way in conversation. For example, you are explaining a concept to someone and you ask them, 'Do you see what I'm saying?' Well, the rich man in this life never saw the kingdom of God. He never realized the glory of the King and the pleasures that are at the right hand of God forever more. He could not see it now in hell either, in a saving way—he is still unregenerate. But in the parable, he is described as at least being aware that there are blessings enjoyed by Lazarus, that he himself is deprived of.

Secondly, he not only saw something of what he had never seen in this life, he felt what he had never felt in this life, at least not to the same degree. His soul was thirsty. He longed for refreshing water to cool his tormented tongue. He apparently never felt that thirst in this life, at least not in any substantial, persistent manner. He had been satisfied to live without God and he had all the temporal pleasures his heart desired. But now his soul is tormented by unfulfilled thirst.

In the Bible spiritual need is often spoken of as a thirst. A felt awareness of need for mercy and pardon, for a new heart, for salvation from sin, a longing for wholeness and purpose, an end to separation from God; all of these are compared to thirst for water. *As the deer pants for the*

water brooks, so pants my soul for You, O God (Psalm 42:1).
Or Psalm 63:1: *O God ... early will I seek You: my soul thirsts
for You, my flesh longs for You in a dry and thirsty land, where
there is no water.*

The gospel invitation goes out in this life to those who
are thirsty for this saving water, calling them to come
to Christ and to drink freely, and God promises to give
this water to all who come. Isaiah 55:1 says *Ho! Everyone
who thirsts, come to the waters.* And again in Isaiah 41:17:
*The poor and needy seek water, but there is none, Their tongues
fail for thirst. I, the LORD, will hear them; I, the God of Israel,
will not forsake them.* Jesus said to the woman at the well,
*Whoever drinks of the water that I shall give him shall never
thirst. But the water that I shall give him will become in him
a fountain of water springing up into everlasting life* (John
4:14). He proclaims the gospel invitation in these words
in John 7:37–38: *If anyone thirsts, let him come to Me and
drink. He who believes in Me, as the Scripture has said, out of
his heart will flow rivers of living water.* Near the end of the
last chapter of the Bible this same gospel invitation is
given again in similar terms: *And the Spirit and the bride
say, 'Come!' And let him who hears say 'Come!' And let him
who thirsts come. Whosoever desires let him take the water of
life freely* (Revelation 22:17). And heaven is described as
a place where John saw *a pure river of water of life, clear as
crystal, proceeding out of the throne of God and of the Lamb*
(Revelation 22:1).

The rich man had never seen what he sees now, nor
felt what he feels now; at least not anywhere close to the

same degree. He was thirsty. Again, remember, Jesus is describing the soul, the spirit, of the man in hell, and he's speaking figuratively. He describes the soul of the rich man as tormented with thirst for water. But there was no hope. There is no water in hell and so none will be given. The rich man could have had the *true* water, the living water of salvation, if he had desired it in this life. If he had felt his need of it, and had sought it from God, he could have had it without money and without price. He could have taken of the water of life freely. If he had only repented and turned to God with faith in Christ, he would have received that true and living water which alone can quench the thirst of the soul, and he would now be in the presence of Christ forever, where that pure river of the water of life flows out from the throne of God. But too late; he is tormented with a kind of thirst, a gnawing, nagging emptiness and torment that will never be quenched.

Thirdly, he did what he had never really done in this life. He prayed and he cried for mercy: *And he cried and said, Father Abraham, have mercy on me.* Probably this was the first truly earnest prayer he had ever uttered. That is not to say he never said prayers. He probably said his prayers many times in this life, maybe even every day. But there's a big difference between saying prayers and really praying. True prayer is the expression of genuine felt desires and longings of the heart, not just the mouthing of words. Now he is earnest in what he is asking for! He really desires to have some water to cool his tormented tongue. If only in a similar way he had sought the *true* water, the living water of Christ, while there was still hope, he wouldn't be in torment. But he never did.

Perhaps this is the case with someone reading these words who has been saying prayers for years, both in public and in private. You know all the right words to use, but you've never really prayed with any real heart's desire and earnest longing for the salvation that is in Christ. You're simply doing what you've been taught to believe is right and pleasing to God, the neglect of which would interfere with your good opinion of yourself and make your conscience uneasy. My friend, do you not realize that saying prayers without praying is a sin? It's taking the name of God in vain! And the Scripture says that, *The LORD will not hold him guiltless who takes His name in vain* (Exodus 20:7). Yet how often this is done in this matter of prayer.

For example, men, women, boys and girls often go to the house of God to worship on the Lord's Day but they go expecting nothing, looking for nothing, and never really asking for anything from God with any real desire and longing. It's just a matter of custom. They go each week to keep their conscience appeased and to see their friends. That's all it really is—they come to the house of prayer and say their prayers but they never really pray.

Perhaps you're reading this and you've never really prayed to God for the salvation of your soul. You've never really cried out to Christ for mercy like a thirsty soul seeking water, or like a hungry soul seeking food, who will not be denied. If you seek him with your whole heart, you'll find him. If you ask it shall be given, if you seek you shall find, if you knock the door will be opened to you. That is Jesus' promise. But you never pray. You're just content to say your prayers and to go through religious motions. Perhaps you don't even do that. I challenge you, not to be harsh, but in the hope of awakening you because I care for your soul. I too was once in such a condition.

The Problem with His Plea

What was the problem with the man's prayer in his torment? To begin with, it was directed to the wrong person: he cried to Abraham and not to God.[8] This is the problem with the prayers of some. They pray to the saints or they pray to mother Mary. It is wrong to do that. Nowhere in the Bible are we commanded, or encouraged, to pray to mother Mary or to the saints. We are to pray to God alone and we are to come to him through his Son, Jesus Christ, who is the *only* Mediator between God and men (1 Timothy 2:5).

Something else was wrong with his prayer: it wasn't the prayer of a truly repenting heart. He desires to have relief from his pain, but we are not to think the man in torment was now a new man, that he was truly ashamed and broken about his sins. He is simply crying for relief from his suffering, but it is too late for that. The opportunity for salvation has passed with the ending of his earthly life.

This points us to something even more fundamental and basic that is wrong with the rich man's prayer. Very simply, it is too late. I wonder if people pray in hell? Certainly, they don't pray with hearts of faith and repentance, but, surely, they must be full of desires for relief from their suffering, as the rich man in torment was. What agonies of soul, what cries and groanings must the damned in hell experience. But all their cries for relief are to no avail, they will never be answered. It is too late.[9]

Lessons

The first lesson I introduce with a question: My friend, do you pray? I'm not asking if you say your prayers. Do you really pray? Can it be said of you, as it was of Paul right after his conversion, *Behold, he is praying*? Do you feel your need of God? Do you feel your need as one who was born into this world without God and is dead in trespasses and sin? Have you ever really felt the need of seeking him and finding him? Are you truly desiring to have that need supplied? Does God know that you truly desire to be saved because he has heard you in that private place, or in your heart, crying to him and asking him to have mercy on your soul, crying to him to pardon your sins for Christ's sake and to give you the Holy Spirit and to make you a new creation in Christ Jesus? Have you cried to God in this way? Are you praying to him really desiring to be saved by Jesus Christ? Does your soul desire to have Christ as your Savior and to become subject to him as the King of kings?

Listen, dear friend, if you know nothing of this, be certain that unless your heart is changed before you die, or before Christ returns, you will go where the rich man went. You will go to hell and, like the rich man, you may cry for relief from the torment but it will be too late. Why not pray now for the true water, the living water? Why not pray for salvation? I beg you! Why not go to Christ now and ask him to save you? Now there is hope. He will hear you when you cry to him. It is not too late, as long as you still have breath. The Scripture says, *And let him who thirsts come. Whoever desires, let him take the water of life freely* (Revelation 22:17). Jesus promises, *the one who comes to Me I will by no means cast out* (John 6:37). Why not look to him and come to him now?

Oh, but someone says, 'My problem is that I don't thirst. My heart is hard and unfeeling. Doubt and skepticism have me in their grip.' Or, 'I'm in bondage to unbelief.' Or, 'my heart is wed to my sins and I can't give them up, even if I tried.' Yes, but Christ can save you from all of this, if you're only willing to be saved by him. He doesn't ask you to save yourself, he invites you to come to him in all your sin and need for him to do for you and in you what you could never do for yourself. When he saves, he not only clears the sinner's bad record, he changes the sinner's bad heart. He can give you the Holy Spirit to make you new. He says, *If anyone thirsts, let him come to Me and drink ... out of his heart will flow rivers of living water.* And we are told that *this He spoke concerning the Spirit, whom those believing in Him would receive* (John 7:37–39). The Scripture says that, even as we who are evil fathers know how to give good gifts to our children, how much more shall the heavenly Father give the Holy Spirit to those who ask him (Luke 11:13).

Do you ask him? He is ready to give the Holy Spirit to those who do. Whoever you are, if you've never repented and believed the gospel and entrusted your soul and your life to Jesus Christ, I exhort you not to despair. But I also exhort you not to trifle with God. Now is the day of salvation; today Christ offers himself to you as your Savior and King. The living water is freely held out to you. Call upon him while he is near, cast yourself in full surrender upon Christ for mercy and he will save you. He has promised to do so. Don't procrastinate any longer.

'But how do I come to him?' You must come to him just as you are. He is there with you, he sees you, he knows you, he hears you. Look to him. Come to him in your heart. Believe his promise. Take the advice of that great preacher of the past, Ralph Erskine:

> Do what you can to fly up to Christ; if you cannot fly, run without wearying; if you cannot run, endeavor to walk without fainting; if you cannot walk because of your broken leg, then creep to the Great Physician with it, and hold out your broken leg, and withered soul to him. He hath not said to the seed of Jacob, 'seek ye me in vain'; if you cannot cry, look to him; [he says] 'Look to me, and be saved, all the ends of the earth'; if you cannot look to him, long for him, for 'he satisfies the longing soul'; sigh and sob and groan after him.

Whatever you do, or however you do it, go to Christ and he will not turn you away. Adopt the prayer of Jacob when he said, *I will not let You go until You bless me* (Genesis 32:26), and he will bless you and he will save you.

Secondly, we are reminded by what we have seen of the cause of prayer too late. Why is it only *after* the rich man was in hell that he finally began to pray for water? Because he was never thirsty like that before. In hell he saw what he had never seen and felt what he had never felt in the same way in this life. At the very least this provides an illustration of what is true of lost sinners in this life. Until they see their spiritual need, and truly see in Christ the only one who can meet their need, they will never cry to him and come to him for salvation.

My dear friend, according to the Scriptures, this is the state of all men by nature. Paul in Ephesians 4:17–18 describes the natural state of man in this way. He says that men in their lost condition, *Walk in the vanity of their mind, having the understanding darkened, being alienated from the life of God through the ignorance that is in them* (KJV). He tells us in 1 Corinthians 2:14 that, *the natural man does not receive the things of the Spirit of God, for they are foolishness to him; nor can he know them.* He tells us in 2 Corinthians 4:4 that, *The god of this world* [Satan] *has blinded the minds of those who believe not, lest the light of the glorious gospel of Christ should shine unto them.* What does all of this tell us? It tells us that unless God the Holy Spirit intervenes and opens the eyes and changes the heart, every man, woman, boy, or girl who has ever lived will remain in their lost condition.

What does this tell us who are Christians? It tells us that we must pray for the lost. We need to pray for the Spirit to be poured out upon all our endeavors to reach the lost. We are totally dependent upon the work of the Holy Spirit. It takes nothing less than a supernatural work of the Spirit of God to awaken spiritually dead sinners and to grant faith in Christ. God must bring the sinner to an awareness of his need and to see his true condition or he will never cry for mercy. We must pray that the Holy Spirit would accompany the preaching of God's Word in and by the church.

If you are not a believer learn that when God the Holy Spirit is troubling your soul you must not try to suppress it or ignore it. Conviction of sin and the fear of hell are great mercies from God. To be uneasy and concerned about your soul is not a bad thing, it is a good thing. God, in mercy, is having dealings with you, friend. Beware of grieving and quenching the Holy Spirit when he comes to deal with your heart. Welcome him, fall in with what he is moving you to do and run to Jesus Christ. Don't go away from these pages and try to forget the things you've been reading. Don't try to smother the voice of God by turning on the TV or connecting to Facebook, or Twitter, or Snapchat. Instead, you should go to your room and get alone with God and have dealings with God about your soul. Conviction of your sin and need is not your enemy, it is your friend. It is intended to lead you to Christ before it is too late. It is better to be briefly miserable and troubled now than to be miserable in the torments of hell for eternity. The Spirit is drawing you to Christ: don't quench him, don't ignore him, don't provoke him to leave you. Welcome him and go to Christ now and give yourself up to him who alone can save you.

Chapter Four

No Escape from Hell

In previous chapters we've been considering the description Jesus gives of the first plea of the man in hell. Now our focus will be on the reply to his plea and the lessons we may learn from it. Abraham's reply has three parts to it: an allusion to privilege, an appeal to memory and an assertion of finality.

An Allusion to Privilege

Abraham said, *Son.* Here, again, we have an allusion to the privileges and opportunities this man neglected. He was a physical son of Abraham. He addressed Abraham in v24 as, *Father Abraham.* As we saw earlier, Jesus is reminding the Jews of his day that you can be of the seed of Abraham according to the flesh and not be of the seed of Abraham according to the Spirit.[10]

What is the application of this to us? It reminds us, again, that religious privilege is not salvation. You can

be a son of the church, and a child of Christian parents;
you can grow up in a home where there are daily family
devotions and in a church where you hear the Word of
God taught by your Sunday School teachers and your
pastors. You can know all of the Bible stories by heart
and memorize your catechism and have all of those
outward privileges, and still be without Christ and go
to hell. Not that these things are bad. They are good!
They are, indeed, great privileges intended to lead you
to Christ. But the privileges of a Christian home and
upbringing alone cannot save you; you must be born
again. You must have a new heart, you must have real
and genuine dealings with Christ for yourself.

Perhaps there is someone reading this who has been
blessed with a Christian upbringing. May I challenge you
gently but seriously with some questions? Have you gone
beyond Mom and Dad and their Christ, so that he has
become your Christ? Have you gone to Jesus for yourself
and said, 'I'm not content merely to be a religious person
or an outwardly nice boy or girl, man or woman. I'm not
content merely to go to church and to learn about the
Bible. I'm not content with those things alone. I want
to be a true Christian. I want Jesus to be my Lord and
my Savior. I want to belong to him. I'm not content that
Mom and Dad should pray for me, I'm going to pray for
myself. I'm not content that the pastors should pray for
my salvation, I'm going to pray for my own salvation.
Lord Jesus, have mercy on me a sinner.' My dear friend,
young or old, have you sought Christ and found him
for yourself? Have you trusted him for yourself? Have

you surrendered yourself to him as your Lord? He is willing to receive you and to save you but you must not be satisfied simply to rest in your religious privileges. You must have Christ for yourself or the memory of all the privileges God has given you will only aggravate your misery in hell. It is not hard to imagine how the bitter memories of opportunities lost and privileges neglected must have stung the conscience of this man in hell when Abraham answered him by calling him 'son.' Yes, you are a son of Abraham but those privileges cannot help you now.

Jesus said in Matthew 11 it would be more tolerable for the people of Sodom and Gomorrah on the Day of Judgment than for the people of Capernaum who had heard him preach. But how could that be? The people of Sodom were guilty of gross sexual perversions and of the foulest forms of flagrant wickedness imaginable, while the people of Capernaum were a religious people. How could Jesus say it would be more tolerable for the people of Sodom on the Day of Judgment than for the people of Capernaum? This is how: the people of Capernaum had rejected the gospel in the context of great privilege and opportunity. They had the Word of God, the priesthood and the temple. They heard Jesus himself preach. But even with all these privileges, they would not repent. We may be assured the inhabitants of Sodom will be in hell. But those religious people of Capernaum who refused to repent, even in the face of such privileges, their hell will be even hotter. *For everyone to whom much is given, from him much will be required; and to whom much has been committed, of him they will ask the more* (Luke 12:48).

My dear unsaved friend who may be reading these pages, perhaps you've heard the gospel and heard it many times. So you have been blessed to sit under the sound of God's Word and to have many opportunities to come to Christ. Do you see it will be more tolerable for Sodom and Gomorrah on the Day of Judgment than for you, if you do not repent? So, there is an allusion to privilege in Abraham's reply. Secondly, there is also ...

An Appeal to Memory

*But Abraham said, 'Son, **remember**'* (v25). This seems to imply that the damned in hell are able to remember, and this, no doubt, is one of their greatest torments. As J.C. Ryle comments, 'The recollection of former things will be one of the worst parts of hell.' But Abraham not only told him to remember, he specifically told him *what* to remember.[11] The man in hell asked for water to cool his tormented tongue. Instead Abraham called him to remember. And what he told him to remember has two parts to it.

First, he said remember in your lifetime you received your good things. Notice carefully the language here. It is not merely good things in and of themselves. It is not merely you received good things in contrast with the bad things Lazarus received. No, the language is you received *your* good things. The idea seems to be that you received those things on earth you considered to be truly good. You made your choice as to what you considered to be the most valuable and desirable things and you sought and received your good things to the neglect of your soul. You cared nothing for Christ and salvation from sin and the glory of God and the kingdom of God. These were not the most valuable things to you. But you received *your* good things. Those things you set your eye upon and pursued and were willing to content yourself with, you received them. You had the finest food, the most stylish clothes, the finest home and you enjoyed the pleasures of sin for a season. These are the things you looked to and trusted in for true happiness, security and wellbeing in life. This is the portion you chose, but the day of your good things is past and you must reap according to what you have sown. You see how true are the words of Christ when he said, *For what will it profit a man if he gains the whole world, and loses his own soul?* (Mark 8:36). Son, remember, that you have already received your good things

How do you think the man viewed those things he once considered as so good, now that he is in torment?[12] How did he view those things now for which he had forfeited his soul, those things he put before Christ and salvation, those darling sins he refused to part with for Christ? Do you think he considered them to be good things now, the most valuable things? Do you think any lost soul in hell believes he made a good bargain by making such things his idols and by living for such things? I don't think so. How painful it must be for the damned in hell to remember the foolish choices they made.

Secondly, he reminds him that 'Lazarus received evil things but now he is comforted and you are tormented'. The word 'evil' is used here in the sense of painful things, or hard things, or difficult things. Sometimes you will find the word evil used in Scripture, not to refer to moral evil, but to calamities and hardships—this is the thought here. While the rich man lived in pleasure, Lazarus was lying at his gate covered in sores. Lazarus lived a life marked by many hardships and sufferings but look at how the tables have turned.

I remind you of what I took some time to point out in an earlier chapter. Jesus is not teaching that the reason Lazarus went to heaven is because he had a difficult life. That's not the point. Remember the rich man went to hell not because he was rich, but because he was unconverted. He lived for this world and would not repent; he was content to live without God and without Christ. Likewise, Lazarus went to heaven, not because he was poor, but because he was a believer. The real point is that our outward condition in this life is not the important thing. It is the state of our soul toward God that is important. It is where we spend eternity that is important. If a man experiences the most horrible sufferings imaginable in this life and yet he spends eternity in heaven after he dies, that man is far better off than the man who enjoys nothing but ease and pleasure in this life and then spends eternity in hell.

Perhaps if he noticed him at all, the rich man, while he was on the earth looked at Lazarus with pity. Perhaps his thoughts were along the lines of, 'that wretched grotesque man with sores all over his body, what good has his faith done him? Look at him. I don't know whether to feel sorry for him or to be disgusted at him.' But the fact is Lazarus possessed a treasure much more valuable than all the rich man's gold, for Christ was his possession and heaven would be his home. The rich man had his good things, but after death he is the one to be pitied because, having rejected Christ, he must suffer the torments of the damned, while Lazarus is comforted.

So, in Abraham's reply to this first plea of the man in hell, there is an allusion to privilege and an appeal to memory. There is also an assertion of finality.

An Assertion of Finality

The pains of hell themselves were unbearable enough. The refusal of his plea for mercy was bad enough. But at least there might still be the hope that just as his good things had come to an end, perhaps the terrible torments and agonies of hell will one day come to an end. Maybe there will be an end to this at some point. If there could be at least a ray of hope that these hell torments would one day end, even if that day were a million years away, there would be something to look forward to.

But Abraham now cuts off any hope of relief. The pleasures of sin are only for a season but the pains of hell will be eternal. There is no escape. He says in v26, *And besides all this, between us and you there is a great gulf fixed, so that those who want to pass from here to you cannot, nor can*

those from there pass to us. The point here is not that hell
and heaven are in the same general location and there
is a big, impassable valley between them. Remember,
Jesus is using figurative language to describe spiritual
reality, so the point is that it is impossible for one's
position to be changed after death. Once in hell, men are
in hell forever.

Granted it might be argued that the eternality of hell
is not necessitated by the picture Jesus draws for us. The
gulf described may only refer to the fact that after death
our state is fixed. The entire case for the eternality of hell
cannot be made from this passage and there are many
who deny the doctrine of eternal punishment for the
lost—there have even been evangelicals who deny this
doctrine. Some argue that after suffering in hell for a
time, eventually those in hell will be released and will go
to heaven, but this is not taught anywhere in the Bible.
Others argue that hell is nothing more than annihilation,
the cessation of personal existence. The fact is, it is
impossible to give full weight to the actual language of
Scripture and draw that conclusion. It is awful to think
about, and it may be a subject we might naturally wish to
avoid. Nevertheless, we need to face what the Scriptures
say to us. Consider the following arguments for the
never-ending suffering of the damned in hell.

First, the Scriptures very often assert that the
sufferings of the damned are *eternal* or *everlasting*. Both
English words are used to translate the same Greek
word. Matthew 18:8 says that the lost will be cast into

everlasting fire; 1 Thessalonians 1:9 speaks of everlasting destruction. Hebrews 6:2 calls it eternal judgment; Jesus speaks of it in Matthew 25 as everlasting punishment. This punishment has no end—the word translated 'everlasting' or 'eternal' means just that.

This is the same word used to describe the eternal existence of God in 1 Timothy 1:17, Romans 1:20 and Romans 16:26. It's the same word used to describe the eternality of Christ (Revelation 1:18), and the eternality of the Holy Spirit (Hebrews 9:14). This is also the same word used to describe the endless duration of the heavenly joys of the redeemed. As long as God exists, and as long as Christ exists, and as long as the Holy Spirit exists, and as long as the joys of the saints in heaven continue, so long, also, is the punishment and torment of the damned in hell.

Secondly, in Scripture the eternal punishment of the damned is set forth as strictly parallel to the eternal blessedness of the saved. Consider what Jesus says in Matthew 25:46, *And these will go away into everlasting punishment: but the righteous into eternal life.* 'Everlasting' and 'eternal' here translate the same Greek word, so here we see that the punishment of the wicked is eternal in just the same way the blessedness of the righteous is eternal. If you wish to deny the one, must you not also deny the other? You cannot have it both ways. We must not deny either, for the Bible teaches both.

Thirdly, the Bible uses other language as well to describe hell pointing to this same truth. *The fire will*

never be quenched (Mark 9:48), Jesus says. This conveys
the idea that what fuels the fire of hell will never be
exhausted, a figurative way of saying that the torments
of hell do not issue in annihilation and thus come to an
end. We are told that the lost *shall be tormented with fire
and brimstone* and that *the smoke of their torment ascends up
forever and ever and they have no rest day or night* (Revelation
14:10–11). How much more clearly could God put it, that
the sufferings of the damned in hell will never end?

I realize this is very graphic and horrifying language.
I do not write these words with some perverse desire
to make things sound worse than they are, or without
feeling the awfulness of what is described, and a sense of
grief at the thought that any of my fellow human beings
should ever have to suffer these things. But, I trust, you
will grant that I am simply setting before you what the
Bible actually says. These first three arguments for the
eternality of hell are taken directly from Scripture.

Fourthly, it can be argued that the eternal duration
of the torments of hell is a moral necessity. Granted
this is an argument from logic, but I think it can be
demonstrated that the eternal duration of the
punishment of sinners is not only biblical, it is rational,
a moral necessity if God is who he is and sin is what it is.

Think with me. Someone says, 'But God is merciful and
kind and full of grace. I just can't accept that a God of
mercy and grace would allow such suffering.' Well, it is
true that God is merciful and kind and full of grace. He
is the God who so loved the world that he gave his only

begotten Son that whoever believes in him should not perish but have eternal life. But what exactly is grace? Grace is God's kindness and love and mercy shown to people who do not deserve it. Grace is not something God owes to anyone. A judge is under no obligation to show mercy to criminals. Mercy is undeserved by its very nature. God has said, *I will have mercy upon whom I will have mercy* (Exodus 33:9; Romans 9:15). But if mercy is obligatory there's no such thing as mercy. If God is indebted to us to give us grace there is no such thing as grace. So, if we wish to argue that God can't punish sinners because God is merciful and gracious, what we're actually doing is eliminating mercy and grace from the whole equation. We are saying that God owes it to sinners not to punish them.

Someone else might say, 'I'm not arguing that it's wrong for God to punish sinners. I just can't see how it can be right for God to punish them so severely as to leave them to suffer in hell for eternity. It's not *just* for God to damn sinners to eternal hell. The punishment is far greater than the crime.' Is it? It may seem that way to us, but is it really?

One problem is that as sinful human beings, we have a tendency to feel that way because we fail to appreciate the glory and the majesty of the God with whom we have to do. We fail to have a proper perception of the infinite evil of sin against such a God. The truth is justice actually demands that hell be eternal.

It is a moral necessity for the torments of hell to be

eternal, because of who God is and what sins against God deserve. In terms of justice, the degree and magnitude of punishment must match the magnitude of the crime. What determines the magnitude of sin? Among other things, the worth and dignity of the person sinned against. We could include the degree of our indebtedness to that person and of their worthiness of our respect and love. In fact, we are so made by God we have an inherent, inbuilt, consciousness of this. That's why we feel a greater shock at the murder of a President than we do at the killing of someone's pet lizard. Or think of it this way, if I spit in your dog's face you might feel that I need to be punished for that in some way. But what if I spit in your mother's face? We all naturally feel, and recognize, that spitting in your mother's face would deserve a much greater punishment than spitting in your dog's face. Why? Because the worth and dignity of your mother is much greater and my obligation to treat her with honor and respect is much greater.

But how do we assess God himself? God is an infinite eternal being, a being of eternal majesty and infinitely limitless worth. As the one who created me and sustains my very life every single moment of every day, and as the one who is the ultimate source of everything lovely and morally pure, my obligation to obey him and to love him and to honor him is an infinite obligation. Therefore, because of who God is and who I am in relation to God, my sins against him are so wicked and evil the punishment they have deserved cannot be exhausted.

Now there will be *degrees* of punishment in hell. The Scripture indicates that in various places. But all will be punished with an *eternal* punishment because sin against God deserves that: no man can render and exhaust the punishment due in a limited space of time.

It may seem illogical to say that all sin against God deserves an eternal punishment and at the same time to speak of degrees of punishment in hell. Jonathan Edwards in one of his sermons addresses this by using the illustration of a line, an infinite line. We might conceive of a line having no end that is also a certain very broad width. We might conceive of another line much narrower in its width but still having no end. Some sins may not be as great as others but they still deserve a punishment that is eternal in duration, though different in degree from others. It is not illogical to conceive of unending punishment but in varying degrees of intensity. The degree of punishment in hell may vary but the duration is the same for all.

No mere man could ever render satisfaction for sins against an eternal and infinite God. Only the God-man could do that, Jesus Christ, because he too is a being of infinite worth. He too is eternal. His suffering humanity was joined to his infinite Deity, rendering his atonement of sufficient worth to atone for all the sins of all who look to him in faith. But no mere man could do what the Lord Jesus Christ did. Because God is just and holy, he must punish sinners, and he must punish them consistent with what their sins actually deserve. Because this is so, sinners will be punished in hell forever. God cannot ignore sin or punish sinners with any punishment less than they deserve without ceasing to be just and holy. For him to do that would be to cease to be God and moral chaos and anarchy would win out and ultimately rule the universe. Because of who God is and what sin is, the eternal duration of hell's torment is a moral necessity. This is a hard truth and there is no way to make it pleasant. Our feelings naturally revolt at this. Partly, as mentioned earlier, this is because even the most morally sensitive of us do not have a full and proper appreciation of the worth, majesty and glory of the God with whom we have to do, or of the evil of even the least sin against him and what it truly deserves.

Then let me add that it can also be argued that the eternal duration of hell is a moral necessity because the damned in hell will never cease from sinning. As we will see in the next chapter, the rich man continued to sin even while he was in hell. The damned in hell will still be unregenerate, they will still have sinful hearts. The whole time they are in hell their sinful lusts and passions will still rage within them and the enmity of their hearts toward God will be given vent. Therefore, as they will continue to sin in hell, they will continue to accrue guilt and to deserve more punishment. As their sinning never ends, so their torment will never end.

But regardless of how we may think about this, it is certain the Bible teaches that the torments of the damned will be eternal. We may or may not understand that, but we can rest assured that what God does is right. Eternal hell is right for those who will not repent and there is soon coming a day when God is going to establish his righteousness and convince the conscience of every man that he has done right. It will be on that day he has appointed, when he will judge the world in righteousness. It will be that day when God will take it into hand to vindicate his injured majesty and to glorify his justice in the damnation of the wicked who have dishonored him and defiled this world he has made, while at the same time he will magnify the glory of his kindness and grace in the salvation of his people. They are people who have deserved the same fate, but he has redeemed them and saved them from their sins by the precious blood of his own dear Son.

In all our thoughts about the eternality of hell, let us remember that the salvation God gives to us sinners in Jesus Christ is wholly an act of grace. By grace we are saved. This means that salvation is given by God to those who do not deserve it, but who deserve the opposite. One of the reasons it is common for men to reject the idea of eternal hell is a failure to appreciate the fact that God does not owe us salvation. If I feel that it would somehow be harsh and unfair for God to damn me, how can I truly understand and appreciate grace? Salvation becomes a debt God owes to us, not a free gift of undeserved kindness. Grace is only received as grace when I'm convinced that I don't deserve it but deserve the opposite.

What if a husband went to his wife on her birthday and said, 'Honey, I have wonderful good news. I purchased for you a gift certificate for a free facial reconstruction at the local plastic surgeon.' How do you think she would respond to that? I suspect she would be offended. Certainly, she would not receive it gladly as good news, even if for some reason she pretended to. It would only be good news if she felt she really needs facial reconstruction because, perhaps, her face has been deformed by an accident or by some other cause, and, therefore, she deeply appreciates her husband's kindness in providing this for her. In a similar way, men and women will never cordially and gladly receive the gospel of God's free grace in Jesus Christ as good news until they have faced and been convinced of the bad news that we are morally deformed sinners deserving nothing from God but eternal wrath.

Often our problem is our failure to see the great evil of sin against God and this is also one of the faults of much modern preaching. There is little preaching on the true nature and exceeding sinfulness of sin. This is one reason the doctrine of hell is so often viewed as unfair and the gospel does not affect hearts as the most wonderful good news that one could ever hear. Where do we see the evil of sin revealed? It is revealed in many ways in the Bible. However, there are two ways in which it is revealed most clearly. First and foremost, the evil of sin is seen in the fact that nothing less than the suffering and death of the very Son of God could ever effectively atone for it. And then, secondly, it is seen in the fact that hell is eternal.

Let us not be deceived, the torments of the damned in hell will last forever and forever. These are not pleasant thoughts, but the Scriptures press these realities upon us and we must reckon with them. We cannot ignore this aspect of Biblical truth: God warns us about this place called hell for our own good. He warns us so we won't go there. *'As I live,' says the Lord God, 'I have no pleasure in the death of the wicked, but that the wicked turn from his way and live. Turn, turn from your evil ways! For why should you die'* (Ezekiel 33:11).

The good news, my friend, is you don't have to go to hell. No matter who you are, no matter what your sins may be, you don't have to go to hell. There is a way of escape. Jesus came into the world to save sinners. The Scripture says, *In this is love, not that we loved God, but that He loved us, and sent His Son to be the propitiation for our sins* (1 John 4:10). What does that word 'propitiation' mean? What does it mean that God in his love sent his Son to be the propitiation for our sins?

The word 'propitiation' refers to that which appeases wrath, that which turns away wrath. Christ in his death was being offered up as a wrath-appeasing sacrifice. He was turning away the terrible wrath of God from those for whom he died. How? The wrath they deserved was poured out upon him as their substitute. God is a God of holiness, justice and wrath against sinners but he is also a God of mercy and love. And here is the dilemma.

How can his mercy toward sinners bring them salvation in a manner that does not compromise his holiness and justice? How can he remove the wrath that is due to them and that justice demands for their sins? This is the great question and the great dilemma the gospel answers. And the answer is the cross of Jesus Christ. It is not that Jesus by his death on the cross was coercing an otherwise unwilling God to show mercy to sinners. The cross did not turn God's wrath into love. No, it was the love of God that provided the propitiation of his own judicial wrath by giving up his Son to endure that wrath and punishment in our place. *In this is love, not that we loved God, but that He loved us and sent His Son to be the propitiation for our sins.* Even while we were enemies Christ died for the ungodly.

Perhaps you ask, how can the sufferings of Christ for just a few hours atone for all the sins of all who put their trust in him; sins the damned in hell will never be able to atone for, for eternity? I remind you again that this one who suffered and died on the cross under the curse of God's wrath was not an ordinary man. He is the God-man. His suffering humanity was inseparably joined to his eternal Deity as God the Son, conveying infinite worth and value to the atonement he made, so that the Scriptures can declare that all who repent and put their trust in him shall be saved. Whoever shall call upon the name of the Lord shall be saved. Whoever believes in him shall not be condemned but shall have everlasting life.

There is one more lesson from Abraham's reply to the

rich man's plea that should be noted. We should learn from this how to assess properly both the pleasures and the pains that come to men in this life. Dear Christian, don't be overly troubled when you see the wicked prosper. Remember the pleasures of the wicked are only temporal but their sorrows will be eternal. Sometimes the wicked do prosper in this life. Things seem to go well for them. They have very few trials and painful disappointments. But remember, the absence of any pain or sorrow in this life is not always a blessing. It can sometimes be the slipperiest slide into hell.

If you are outside of Christ and continue so, God may let you have *your* good things—those things you desire in this life and are willing to sell Christ and heaven in order to have them. God may let you have them, but remember, *what does it profit a man, if he shall gain the whole world, and lose his own soul?* Those pleasures will only last a short time, while there is an eternity of sorrow awaiting those determined to cling to their sins and reject Christ. Don't think God smiles upon you in your sin simply because everything is going well for you right now. The fact is there is no greater object of pity than the man God leaves at peace in his sin.

I address myself again to believers. Not only should you not be too troubled when you see the wicked prosper in this life, you should also not be overly troubled when you, as a Christian, experience tribulation in this life. Just as the pleasures of the wicked are only temporal but their sorrows will be eternal, remember, the sorrows of the child of God are only temporal, but our joys will be everlasting. As Peter writes, *In this you greatly rejoice, though now for a little while, if need be, you have been grieved by various trials* (1 Peter 1:6). When you are tempted to give up and to give in and to go back to the world, remember these trials are, indeed, only for a season. As Peter goes on to say, the trial of your faith has as its purpose that it might be found unto praise and honor and glory at the appearing of Jesus Christ. As Paul writes in Romans 8:18, *For I reckon that the sufferings of this present time are not worthy to be compared with the glory which shall be revealed in us.*

So, press on, dear brother and dear sister. Do not let appearances fool you. We walk by faith and not by sight. In bad days, and in good, remember the best is yet to come. This world is not our home: we are pressing on toward a city whose builder and maker is God. All our pains and sorrows are temporal. They have an end. Our joys when we see our Lord's face will be eternal. Satan buffets you now but he will buffet you no more then. The battle with remaining sin grieves you and vexes your heart now. But then, there will be no more sin, no more temptation to be resisted, no more of the tears of repentance, no more of the tears of grief over holy desires unfulfilled. Affliction may have come upon you now, but then there will be no more pain, no more sorrow and no more tears. These troubles are only temporal. Our joys will be eternal. Bless his holy name!

Chapter Five

The Scriptures: Sufficient and Self-Authenticating

In the last chapter we considered the first request of the man in torment and Abraham's response to it. Now in Luke 16:27–31 we have the second plea, or the second request, of this man. In the response given to his second request the Lord Jesus is underscoring for us another very important lesson; here we have a powerful affirmation of the sufficiency and self-authenticating nature of Scripture.

The Final Request of the Man in Hell

His first request, back in v.24, was that Lazarus might come to him with a drop of water to cool his tormented tongue. This being denied he comes back now with a second request, *Then he said, I beg you, therefore, father, that you would send him* [Lazarus] *to my father's house.*

Seeing that all of my crying for mercy is of no avail, it is too late, my damnation is final and irrevocable and my punishment will have no end, let me ask about my family. Could not something be done to keep the rest of my family from coming to this awful place of torment?

Then he comes up with a plan, a plan for evangelism. People often do that, don't they? Here is the rich man's plan: I beg you send Lazarus back to my father's house to warn them: v28, *For I have five brethren; that he may testify to them, lest they also come into this place of torment.* So, here is his plan for effective evangelism: send Lazarus back from the dead to warn them.

Now think about this request a moment, because there is an assumption here. The text does not specifically state it, but I think his conversation with Abraham following after this confirms that the request of the rich man in hell involved, to some degree, a subtle kind of self-justification.

Allow me to use an illustration I heard or read, although I can't remember from whom or where! Imagine someone driving down a highway. They come to a sign marking a speed zone and there is a yellow light blinking, indicating that drivers are to slow down to 35mph. However, this driver just plows right on through at 60mph and gets pulled over by a cop assigned to watch the area. As the cop comes up to the car to write the ticket, the driver says, 'You know I have several friends who regularly drive down this road and I don't want them to get a ticket like me. Perhaps you should put up two blinking yellow lights instead of one. I also think the county ought to put up bigger signs warning about the speed zone.' What is the driver really saying? What is he really doing by asking that the highway department put up two lights there, or put up a bigger light or sign, so his friends do not get a ticket? One thing he is doing is making an excuse for himself, implying that he is not fully responsible for his violation. The signs are not big enough, the lights are not bright enough. The fault is with the sign or the lights, not with him. Well, you see, that is exactly what the man in hell is implying by his request—it is nothing less than a subtle form of self-justification. Here he is in hell and no one ever came from the dead to warn him. If only someone had, he wouldn't be here. 'It's really not my fault. It's God's fault. I was never sufficiently warned. Do what was never done for me and give sufficient warning to my brothers by sending Lazarus back from the dead to tell them firsthand what he has seen.' This, I'm convinced, is the real spirit, or at least a large element of the spirit, of the rich man's request. This will become even clearer in a few moments.

Well, what was Abraham's response? It is very simple and brief: *Abraham said to him, 'They have Moses and the prophets; let them hear them'* (v.29). This expression (Moses and the prophets) was a common way of referring to *the writings* of Moses and the prophets, or as we would say, the Old Testament Scriptures. Abraham is saying the Scriptures are enough. The Scriptures are sufficient to warn men of everlasting punishment and to point them to the way of salvation. Let them hear the Scriptures. So, we have this second request of the man in hell and Abraham's reply. Next, we have the protest of the man in hell.

The Protest of the Man in Hell

How did the rich man respond to Abraham's words? He raises a protest. This contempt for God's Word that he had shown while on earth, has followed him into hell. He hasn't changed. He raises a protest in hell.

His Argument

And he said, 'No, father Abraham' (v.30). No, father Abraham, I am sorry but you're wrong. True, they have the Scriptures but that is not enough. If someone goes to them from the dead, then they will repent, then they will be persuaded. That will do it, that is what is needed. The Scriptures alone are not enough. They were not enough for me and they are not enough for them. Let some great miracle be performed, show them a sign and they will believe. Let Lazarus return from glory to authenticate the message of Scripture. When this visitor from beyond the grave tells them about hell and about heaven, the spectacular and unusual manner of the warning, and the terror of his appearance, will alarm them and awaken them. When they see Lazarus, they will be so struck with fear and awe, they will be convinced, persuaded, and they will repent. The Scriptures are not enough, but if one comes to them from the dead, that will do it. This is his argument.

Its Refutation

Abraham refutes this man's protest. This is the climax of this entire parable, *But he said to him, 'If they do not hear Moses and the prophets, neither will they be persuaded though one rise from the dead* (v.31). What is Jesus saying to us here through the mouth of Abraham? He is telling us that, not only are the Scriptures sufficient, but that there is no other means better, or more effective, than the Scriptures. The God who has made us knows better than we do what is most adapted to bring men to repentance. He who has made all the faculties of our souls knows how to speak best to men. He has chosen his Word, the Scriptures, to be accompanied by the awakening and renewing influences of the Holy Spirit and thus have saving power. If men will not hear the Scriptures, if that is not enough for them, they have no hope of being persuaded by any other means. *If they do not hear Moses and the prophets, neither will they be persuaded though one rise from the dead.*

This has some very important implications with reference to our entire view of the Bible, particularly in its relationship to the salvation of men. I want to underscore two important truths that are here and seek to draw out some practical lessons from them.

The Scriptures Are Entirely Sufficient to Bring Men to Repentance and Faith in Christ

Now the reference here is specifically to the Old Testament Scriptures, Moses and the Prophets, because only the Old Testament Scriptures were in existence at that time. It is correct to say that at every given point in redemptive history the revelation God gave at that time was sufficient for that time. But if the Old Testament Scriptures were sufficient for the rich man in hell, *how much more* is this true now that Christ, God's final Word, has come? The work of redemption has been finished once and for all and, with the ministry of Christ's authorized and appointed apostles, the canon of Scripture is complete. Now we have *both* the Old and the New Testament Scriptures.

It is the Scriptures which contain the divine law which convicts of sin and judgment and tells us how God requires us to live. And it is the Scriptures which set forth the gospel by which men can be delivered from the guilt and bondage of sin, saved from hell and brought safely to heaven; the gospel that centers in the person and work of the Lord Jesus Christ. As we read in Revelation 19:10, *The testimony of Jesus is the spirit of prophecy.* The whole of Scripture has as its primary focus and purpose the revelation of Jesus Christ and the way of salvation in him.

This is not only true of the New Testament; this is true of the Old Testament as well. Jesus could say to the Pharisees, speaking of the Old Testament Scriptures, *Search the Scriptures ... these are they which testify of me* (John 5:39). We read of Jesus, speaking to the disciples on the road to Emmaus and are told, *Beginning at Moses and all the prophets, He expounded to them in all the Scriptures the things concerning Himself* (Luke 24:27). We read of him saying to his disciples in the upper room, *These are the words which I spoke to you while I was still with you, that all things must be fulfilled which were written in the law of Moses and the Prophets and the Psalms concerning Me* (Luke 24:44). Concerning me! Peter could declare to the house of Cornelius, *To Him all the prophets witness that, through His name, whoever believes in Him will receive remission of sins* (Acts 10:43). This is not some new message unique to New Testament times. The message of Scripture is one, found in both the New and the Old Testaments. To *this truth* Peter says, all the prophets bear witness. What truth? The truth that through his name, through the name of Jesus Christ, whoever believes in him shall receive remission of sins.

In the Old Testament, we have Christ revealed in the unfolding of God's covenant promise, in the predictions, in the types, in the sacrificial system of worship. We have him revealed in the prophecies describing virtually every aspect of his work, from the place and nature of his birth, to the horrible manner and meaning of his death, to the glory of his resurrection, ascension and exaltation. All these things about Christ are revealed in the Old Testament Scriptures.

Then in these New Testament days what was revealed in the Old by means of shadows and types, promises and prophecies is much more clearly revealed and seen in the blazing light of fulfillment. We see in the gospels Jesus born of a virgin, Jesus going about doing good and teaching the people the will of God. We see Jesus suffering and dying upon the cross in the place of sinners. We see him raised from the dead and ascending to the right hand of the Father. Think about that! The fact is, someone has come back from the dead. Jesus Christ was raised from the dead by which his claims to be the Son of God were vindicated. Furthermore, his resurrection was confirmed by numerous eyewitnesses, many of whom died a martyr's death rather than to deny what they knew to be true. In the New Testament epistles we see him, and this great salvation, further explained and applied to the lives of his people. We hear of the glory that is yet to come when he returns to this world a second time to judge the world in righteousness and to bless his people. This is the message of the Bible.

So, Jesus in this account of Lazarus and the rich man, underscores that the Scriptures, our Bibles, are fully adequate and sufficient to bring men to repentance and faith in him.

Send back Lazarus to my Father's house to warn my brothers.

They have the Scriptures, is Abraham's reply, *let them hear them.*

No, father Abraham, that's not sufficient, the Scriptures are inadequate. If someone went back from the dead, they would repent.'

You are wrong, is Abraham's answer, *if they will not hear the Scriptures neither will they be persuaded, though one rise from the dead.*

What is the message? The message is very simply this: the Scriptures are enough. The Scriptures are fully adequate. The Scriptures are completely sufficient for salvation.

Now all of us need to ask ourselves, 'Do I agree with Abraham?' When it comes to the salvation of sinners, Abraham says, or more properly, Jesus says through Abraham, the Scriptures are enough. The rich man in hell says they are not enough. Men need something more than the Scriptures, if they're going to be saved from hell. So which side of the debate are you on? It is a debate that's continued to this present day.

For example, *Roman Catholicism* says the Scriptures are not enough for salvation. We also need the sacred traditions authorized by the Roman church. These are equally authoritative and necessary for faith and salvation. The *Quakers* say the Scriptures are not enough. We need the inner light, an inner voice from God speaking to us. *Theological liberals* say the Scriptures are not enough. The Scriptures must be subjected to the supreme authority of human reason and naturalistic philosophy. Many *charismatics*, in effect, say the Bible is not enough. It has to be supplemented by personal revelations. For much of *the evangelical church* today it increasingly seems that the Scriptures are not enough. We are told that we cannot expect people to read the Bible or to listen to sermons or Bible teaching, that is no good anymore. Folks will never be attracted to that. If we want to reach people, we need concerts and dramas and movies and bands and choreography and celebrities. But Jesus says the Scriptures are enough. The Scriptures are sufficient for salvation.[13]

Perhaps there are fellow pastors reading these pages. My brothers, we need to be confident in the Scriptures. We are reminded here that true evangelism must focus on explaining and applying the truths of God's Word. Some of you may have read the classic work by J.I Packer, *Evangelism and the Sovereignty of God*. He addresses in some detail this very point. He says,

> So, in the last analysis, there is only one method of evangelism: namely the faithful explanation and application of the gospel message. From which it follows ... that the test for any proposed strategy or technique or style, of evangelistic action must be this: will it in fact serve the word? Is it calculated to be a means of explaining the gospel truly and fully and applying it deeply and exactly.

Faith comes by hearing, and hearing by the word of God (Romans 10:17). You see, saving faith presupposes a knowledge of the truth, the truth about God and about man in his sin and about Christ the only Savior. If a person is going to truly believe in Christ, he has to know who Christ is. If he is going to believe the gospel, he has to come, at least, to a basic understanding of the gospel. Faith is not a leap in the dark, it is not ignorance trying to keep up a positive outlook on life. It is not faith in faith, but rather it is faith in Jesus Christ, his person and his work, as revealed in *the Scriptures*.

You may have heard of the man who, when asked what he believed, said, 'I believe what the church believes.' So it was asked, 'What does the church believe?' 'Oh', he said, 'the church believes what I believe.' 'Well then, could you please tell me, what do you and the church believe?' 'We both believe the same thing.' That kind of faith will not do because it is not faith at all, it is ignorance. James Boice mentions a story once told by Harry Ironside about the flamboyant evangelist called Gypsy Smith. He got his name because he really did have a gypsy background and he told lots of fascinating stories about growing up in a gypsy camp. Ironside went to hear him and on this occasion Gypsy Smith's sermon was made up almost entirely of these stories. Yet at the end of the meeting, he gave an altar call, and hundreds of people came streaming forward. Ironside said he wondered what they were coming forward for. 'Perhaps', he said, 'they wanted to become gypsies.'

There is no saving faith unless the message of the gospel is heard and understood. That is our job as ministers of the gospel—not to entertain, not merely to get people to like us or to just get people in and fill up the pews. Our calling, when it comes to the salvation of sinners, is to make Christ known as he is revealed in the Holy Scriptures.

Perhaps someone would like to take exception to this. Maybe someone reading this is thinking, 'I actually sympathize with the rich man's argument.' If that is you, imagine Lazarus did come back from the dead. How would the rich man's brothers have responded? I think it is very possible they would have questioned Lazarus' credibility. 'How do we know this is really Lazarus? Perhaps, we are just hallucinating or someone is trying to trick us.' Remember, my friend, someone did rise from the dead, the Lord Jesus Christ himself and the Jewish rulers tried to dismiss it. Also consider, if Lazarus came back from the dead he could tell the rich man's brothers nothing more than the Bible already told them. I can also imagine that if Lazarus began to tell them that their brother was in hell and that he had been sent back to warn them, they would actually have become angry at him. 'How dare you say that our brother is in hell!' They would probably accuse him of slandering the good name of their deceased sibling.

You see, man in his sin will always find a way to escape the force of truth unless God does a work of sovereign regeneration in his heart. The Scriptures are fully sufficient but if we reject the Scriptures, if the Word of God is not enough for me, the problem is not with the means God has appointed, the problem is with my own heart. Men do not believe because they will not believe. And if they will not be brought to repentance by the Scriptures, there is nothing else in hell, heaven or earth that will ever do it.

Christians, this is why our efforts to preach the gospel must be accompanied by prayer. Unless the Spirit of God comes and renews the heart and overcomes a person's natural blindness and resistance to the truth, the sinner will never come to Christ. We must be people of prayer and our churches must be praying churches. The temptation will always be to try something different. When things seem dry and there are few conversions we can begin to doubt and to think that maybe the gospel is not enough after all. We think we need to try something else to reach people.

Admittedly, there are a lot of things that can get people into our church buildings and fill up the pews, if that is all we are after. But there is only one thing that will save them and that is the gospel of Jesus Christ heard, understood and believingly embraced. This will only occur when the gospel comes to them not in word only, but also in the power of the Holy Spirit. It is not more gimmicks we need, or a new message or means; the problem is the human heart, the unbelief of which will only be overcome by the regenerating work of the Spirit. We must preach and pray, share the gospel and pray. Plead for God with men and plead with God for men. And if the thought should ever rise up in our hearts that the Bible alone, with prayer for the Spirit, is not sufficient to make men wise unto salvation, remember where that thought has its origin. It finds its source in hell.[14]

There is a second very important and related truth contained in Abraham's reply to the rich's man second plea and his protest. Not only are the Scriptures sufficient to bring men to salvation ...

The Scriptures are Sufficiently Self-Authenticating

By self-authenticating we mean self-proving. That which is self-authenticating proves its own authority apart from the need of anything outside of itself to authenticate it.

Let me explain: what was really the essence of the rich man's argument? He was not saying the Scriptures are untrue, in fact he is now painfully aware the Scriptures are true. His argument is that men need something else outside of the Scriptures to convince them the Scriptures are true. Men cannot be expected to believe on the testimony of the Scriptures alone. They need some kind of miracle, or some revelation, or some authority other than and outside of the Scriptures, to convince them that the Scriptures really are the Word of God. The Scriptures by themselves are not able to do that. This is really the essence of his argument.

What was Abraham's response? Abraham says, in effect, not only are the Scriptures true, the Scriptures sufficiently prove themselves to be true. The Scriptures authenticate themselves. The Scriptures in and of themselves sufficiently compel belief in their own authority and trustworthiness. And they do this without any need for something outside of them to authenticate them. If a man has the Scriptures he has enough to be convinced.

This is a very important doctrine. Right here is the very heart of the difference between the Roman Catholic view of Scripture and the Reformed and Protestant view of Scripture. When the question is asked, 'How do we know and believe that the Scriptures are the authoritative Word of God?', Rome argues that it is because the church tells us they are. According to Rome, the Scriptures alone are not enough to compel our faith. The Bible needs something else outside of itself to attest to its divine authority and that something else is the church. It is the consensus of the church, the traditions of the church, the opinions of the Fathers and the declarations of the Pope that authenticate the Scriptures. Therefore, the Roman Catholic Church is, in fact, demanding faith in itself as the final authority, not the Word of God. We are told to believe the Scriptures, not on the authority of God alone, but on the authority of the church. It's the church that authenticates Scripture. This is the Roman Catholic position.

But if that were the case then we would be faced with another question: who authenticates the church? How are we assured the church is trustworthy? This questioning could go on *ad infinitum*, because if some authority authenticates the church, we could ask who authenticates that authority. This has to stop somewhere, with a final and ultimate authority. The doctrine of the Reformation is the very doctrine we see set forth by the Lord Jesus in this text. The Scriptures authenticate themselves. There is no higher authority to which we can appeal than the Scriptures. We believe the Scriptures, not because the church tells us what to believe, or because some outside source authenticates

the Scriptures for us. We believe the Scriptures because
the Scriptures are, in fact, the Word of God, because
the Bible is the very word of the living God speaking to
the creatures he has made; the Scriptures authenticate
themselves.

Now this is not to deny the important role of the
church and its teachers. The Reformed doctrine of the
sufficiency and self-authentication of Scripture does
not exclude the teaching ministry of the church, both
past and present. It does not mean that using other
resources that can help us to understand the Scriptures,
such as good commentaries or works of theology, is
wrong. It does not mean we are to ignore the labors of
the church throughout the centuries to carefully state
and summarize the doctrines of Scripture in creeds
or confessions of faith. Sadly, some evangelicals have
followed in the steps of Alexander Campbell, who said,
'I have endeavored to read the Scriptures as though no
one had read them before me.' That may sound pious,
but it doesn't preserve *sola Scriptura*, it distorts it.[15]
Instead of the Scriptures alone, it becomes me alone. It
is not a denial of the sufficiency of Scripture, or the self-
authenticating nature of Scripture, to be helped in our
understanding of Scripture by others. This is one of the
purposes of the Christian ministry.

The reformers never rejected theological tradition as
bad in and of itself, but only when it could be shown to
contradict Scripture. In the matter of the authentication
of the authority of Scripture, they argued that the

Scriptures are ultimately self-authenticating. The Bible itself is sufficient to compel belief in its own authority. God's Word is not a dead word. It is the Word of the living God, who knows how to speak convincingly to us and, in fact, does so. The Reformed doctrine of the self-authenticating nature of Scripture is well summarized in the language of both the Westminster and Second London Baptist Confessions of Faith which read:

> The heavenliness of the matter, the efficacy of the doctrine, and the majesty of the style, the consent of all the parts, the scope of the whole which is to give glory to God, the full discovery it makes of the only way of man's salvation, and many other incomparable excellencies and entire perfections thereof, are arguments by which it does abundantly evidence itself to be the Word of God.

John Calvin made this point in a very striking way:

> But with regard to the question, 'How shall we be persuaded of its divine original [or origin], unless we have recourse to the decree of the church?' this is just as if anyone should enquire, 'How shall we learn to distinguish light from darkness, white from black, sweet from bitter?' For the Scripture exhibits as clear evidence of its truth, as white and black things do of their color, or sweet and bitter things of their taste.

Someone may ask, 'But if the Scriptures are self-authenticating why doesn't everyone who hears the gospel believe and be saved?' That is a very good question. When men refuse to believe the Scriptures, the problem is not that the Scriptures alone are insufficient to compel belief. It is not that the Scriptures fail adequately to attest to their own authority. It is not that God mumbled and stumbled and has failed to speak to us in a sufficiently clear and convincing manner. The problem is with the sinful bias of the human heart. Men, by nature, willfully refuse to listen and receive the voice of their Creator speaking to them because they do not like what he has to say. We willfully shut our eyes against the truth, *suppressing[ing] the truth in unrighteousness* (Romans 1:18), unless the Holy Spirit does a work of regeneration in our hearts.

Therefore, both the Westminster and Second London Baptist Confessions go on to say, after emphasizing the self-authenticating nature of Scripture:

> Yet notwithstanding, our full persuasion and assurance of the infallible truth and divine authority thereof, is from the inward work of the Holy Spirit bearing witness by and with the Word in our hearts.

This is why Jesus said, *You must be born again*, or you will never see and never enter the Kingdom. The word must come not *in word only, but also in power, and in the Holy Spirit and in much assurance* (1 Thessalonians 1:5). Not the Spirit without the Word, but the Spirit bearing witness by and with the Word in the sinner's heart. It is the Holy Spirit working with the Word who creates faith and opens the heart to embrace the Bible for what it is, the authoritative Word of the living God. The Holy Spirit doesn't make it the Word of God. It is the Word of

God and it sufficiently evidences itself to be. But because man is blinded and prejudiced against the truth in his sin, it is necessary that the Spirit comes in the context of the hearing or reading of God's Word, and when he does his gracious work in the heart of the sinner, the sinful prejudices of his heart are subdued. The soul now sees and is convinced of what was already clear and true all along, not by some outside testimony, not by sophisticated philosophical arguments for the existence of God, not by some kind of external evidence being added to them, but because the Scriptures authenticate themselves to his heart.

Practical Implications

This has tremendous implications for our whole approach to evangelism and apologetics. The main problem is not that we need to come up with some kind of foolproof philosophical argument for God, and then we can sit down with the unbeliever, or the agnostic, or the so-called atheist and, with an unbiased mind, he can weigh the evidence. We want to put God on the examining table, God the specimen, to see if this God and his Word meet up to our standards of proof as we examine him with our supposedly unbiased minds. The problem is that there is no such thing as an unregenerate sinner with an unbiased mind. Man's unbelief is not merely an intellectual problem, it is a moral problem. Scripture says they believe not the truth *because they love not the truth* that they might be saved (2 Thessalonians 2:10). Paul adds that they believe not the truth because they have pleasure in unrighteousness. Jesus said, *This is the condemnation, that light is come into the world, and men loved darkness rather than light, because their deeds were evil* (John 3:19). The problem is not that the Scriptures are somehow lacking and insufficient to compel our faith. The problem is with the human heart. And we must remember, what is the means God's Spirit employs to open the sinner's heart and to give him faith? It is not something outside of the Scriptures; it is the very same Scriptures that people refuse to believe.

Therefore, the best defense of the faith is the positive, authoritative, Spirit empowered, proclamation of God's Word. You do not have to be an expert in archaeology. You do not have to be an expert in philosophy to be a witness for Christ to an unbelieving world, though these things have their place and benefit. Just take the self-authenticating Word of God and proclaim it and get it out. The Word of God is described as a sword that pierces into the soul. It is described as a mirror that reveals to men the truth about themselves, a lamp that shines in the darkness. It is described as a hammer that can break the hardest heart. We must be confident in Holy Scripture and take it and proclaim it and apply it and open up its teaching and expose people to it. We must get it out into the community. We must spread it abroad throughout the world with the unshakeable confidence that the gospel is the power of God unto salvation (Romans 1:16).

When you read about the terrible spiritual conditions

in England before the eighteenth-century Evangelical Awakening, it is not that there were no earnest efforts to stem the tide of degeneration in the church and society. A man named John Conybeare published his *Defense of Revealed Religion* in 1732. Bishop Butler wrote his *Analogy* defending biblical morality and religion in 1736. These were both very learned works, and there were other efforts like this, but they had no effect. For one thing, few people had the mental capacity to study these works, much less to understand them. But what was it that stemmed the tide and brought revival? In the words of J.C. Ryle, the means by which the awakening was commenced and carried on 'was of the simplest description. It was neither more nor less than the old apostolic weapon of preaching.' God raised up a generation of preachers, men like George Whitefield, the Wesleys, William Grimshaw, William Romaine, Daniel Rowland, Howell Harris and many others. These were men who had been born again themselves, who had personal experience of the power of God's Word within their own souls. They loved Jesus Christ, were full of the Holy Spirit and possessed with an undoubted Spirit-given confidence in the sufficiency of Scripture.

Charles Spurgeon once said it this way in a sermon called 'Christ and His Co-workers':

> A great many learned men are defending the gospel; no doubt it is a very proper and right thing to do, yet I always notice that, when there are most books of that kind, it is because the gospel itself is not being preached. Suppose

a number of persons were to take it into their heads that they had to defend a lion. There he is in the cage, and here come all the soldiers of the army to fight for him. Well, I should suggest to them, if they would not object, and feel that it was humbling to them, that they should kindly stand back, and open the door, and let the lion out! I believe that would be the best way of defending him, for he would take care of himself; and the best 'apology' for the gospel is to let the gospel out. Never mind defending Deuteronomy or the whole of the Pentateuch; preach Jesus Christ and him crucified. Let the Lion out, and see who will dare to approach him. The Lion of the tribe of Judah will soon drive away all of his adversaries.

The Word of God is sufficient for salvation and it is self-authenticating. May God help us, as Spurgeon exhorts us, to let the lion out.

Endnotes

1. John Blanchard, *Whatever Happened to Hell?*, Evangelical Press 1993

2. Robert A Peterson, *Hell On Trial: the case for eternal punishment*, P&R 1995

3. JC Ryle, *Expository Thoughts on Luke*, Banner of Truth 1986

4. Brownlow North, *The Rich Man and Lazarus: an exposition of Luke 16:19–31*, Banner of Truth 1979.

5. North, *The Rich Man and Lazarus*, p. 28.

6. All of the preceding quotations are from *Whatever Happened to Hell*, pp. 13–14.

7. Blanchard, *Whatever Happened to Hell?*, p. 156.

8. North, *The Rich Man and Lazarus*, p. 70.

9. North, *The Rich Man and Lazarus*, p. 79.

10. North, *The Rich Man and Lazarus*, p. 87–92.

11. North, *The Rich Man and Lazarus*, p. 95.

12. North, *The Rich Man and Lazarus*, p. 95.

13. Parts of this paragraph adapted from a sermon of Geoff Thomas, The Rich Man and Lazarus 3, accessed at http://www.alfredplacechurch.org.uk/index.php/sermons/luke1/chapter-16/1627-31-the-rich-man-and-lazarus-3/

14. North, *The Rich Man and Lazarus*, p113.

15. Matthew Barret, *God's Word Alone: The Authority of Scripture, What the Reformers Taught ... and Why it Still Matters* (Grand Rapids, Michigan: Zondervan, 2016), p345.